Eventually our adult children leave the nest (we hope). But often we are not prepared for how this transition will affect us. For every parent who is anticipating or experiencing the empty nest, this book is a must-read.

—GARY CHAPMAN, PhD, author, *The Five Love Languages*

This is the perfect sequel to Jim Burns' book *Doing Life with Your Adult Children*. If you find yourself in the empty nest or getting ready to enter it, there is great advice on every page.

—PAT WILLIAMS, Basketball Hall of Famer;
author, *Every Day Is Game Day*

With a paucity of good advice available on the adjustments and losses we experience during this period of life, it is a real blessing to have someone offering help that really works. Thank you, Jim, for writing this remarkable book.

—MEG MEEKER, MD, author, bestselling
Strong Fathers, Strong Daughters

Whether you're single or married, this book will provide the insight, wisdom, and practical advice for you to flourish when your kids leave home. I highly recommend it!

—CHIP INGRAM, CEO and teaching pastor,
Living on the Edge; author, *I Choose Peace*

If you have an empty nest, buy this book! Jim Burns knows what he writes about. His book is full of practical, powerful wisdom—with a dose of humor. Yes, it's a great book!

—RUTH GRAHAM, speaker; Christian evangelist; author,
Transforming Loneliness and *In Every Pew Sits a Broken Heart*

This book is intelligent, researched, inspiring, engaging, and life changing. The wisdom in its pages reflects the heart of a seasoned leader who has spent a lifetime investing in families.

—REGGIE JOINER, CEO and founder, Orange, a division of the
Rethink Group Inc.; author, speaker, and family ministry expert

Jim Burns removes the "empty" from the nest and fills up the space with great compassion, biblical concepts, stories, solutions, and ideas. This is a great sequel to his *Doing Life with Your Adult Children*.

—JOHN TOWNSEND, author, bestselling Boundaries book series;
founder, Townsend Institute for Leadership and Counseling

This is the book we've been waiting for! It is like having a conversation with a trusted friend who's been there and who knows how to help. The best really can be yet to come!

—JODIE BERNDT, author, bestselling *Praying
the Scriptures for Your Adult Children*

The word that most describes the transition into the empty nest is *disorienting*. Jim Burns is a wise and trustworthy guide through this new chapter in your life. The counsel he provides in this book is gold.

—BOB LEPINE, author, *Love Like You Mean It*; cohost, *FamilyLife Today*

Jim Burns' exceptional and practical wisdom is apparent again in this book. It thoroughly guides parents to thrive in this stage of life, and I give it my highest recommendation.

—LARRY FOWLER, founder, Legacy Coalition

I'm all too familiar with the emotions that come when we're facing an empty nest. Jim Burns has been through it too, and he has a wealth of wisdom and encouragement to share.

—JIM DALY, president, Focus on the Family

Jim Burns is smart, witty, grounded, and immeasurably practical. Whether you're getting close to the second half of marriage or are in the thick of it, you won't want to miss out on this fantastic book.

—DRS. LES AND LESLIE PARROTT, authors, bestselling *Saving Your Marriage before It Starts*

Bringing children into your nest changes your life immensely; having them all leave changes your life just as much. You need this book. Nan and I loved Jim's wisdom and perspective. Get ready to thrive in the next season of your life.

—RON DEAL, family therapist; conference speaker; coauthor, bestselling *Building Love Together in Blended Families*

Your best years are ahead of you! That's the message you need to hear, and it rings through every page of this excellent guide. Just as with every book Jim writes, it provides the powerful and practical ideas you need for an even better faith, family, friendships, and future.

—KARA POWELL, chief of leadership formation, Fuller Seminary; coauthor, *Three Big Questions That Change Every Teenager*

The increase in the divorce rate of couples over fifty is a result of painful emptiness. Jim gives every couple or single a dynamic plan to prepare for and experience their best years after the kids are out of the house. Married? Single? Over fifty? Kids gone? This book will help!

—STEVE ARTERBURN, bestselling author; founder, New Life Live!

Finding Joy in the Empty Nest is the definitive book on this subject. I will hand it out to all my friends who are about to enter the empty nest. Jim's warm, authentic, and ever so helpful style makes this a great read.

—DOUG FIELDS, cofounder, Download Youth Ministry; youth pastor; bestselling author

Jim has written an outstanding book designed to help us navigate this important season of life. This is such a wonderful resource for anyone in the empty nest or about to enter it.

—PHILIP AND HOLLY WAGNER, founding pastors,
Oasis Church LA; founders, Generosity.org

This book is a blessing! It reminds empty nesters that we can embrace a fresh start and have a renewed vision to add new purpose and passion into our lives, as well as stay on course for the encore years.

—CHARLOTTE GUEST, *The Empty Nest Guest Podcast*

FINDING JOY
IN THE
EMPTY NEST

DISCOVER PURPOSE AND PASSION
IN THE NEXT PHASE OF LIFE

JIM BURNS

ZONDERVAN
BOOKS

ZONDERVAN BOOKS

Finding Joy in the Empty Nest
Copyright © 2022 by Jim Burns

Requests for information should be addressed to:
Zondervan, *3900 Sparks Dr. SE, Grand Rapids, Michigan 49546*

Zondervan titles may be purchased in bulk for educational, business, fundraising, or sales promotional use. For information, please email SpecialMarkets@Zondervan.com.

ISBN 978-0-310-36264-7 (audio)

Library of Congress Cataloging-in-Publication Data

Names: Burns, Jim, 1953– author.
Title: Finding joy in the empty nest : discover purpose and passion in the next phase of life / Jim Burns.
Description: Grand Rapids : Zondervan, 2022. | Includes bibliographical references. | Summary: "If you're one of the millions of adults struggling with the grief and complex considerations of living in an empty nest, author and motivational speaker Jim Burns's much-anticipated Finding Joy in the Empty Nest will remind you that—with some practical guidance—your second half could very well become your best half"—Provided by publisher.
Identifiers: LCCN 2021041557 (print) | LCCN 2021041558 (ebook) | ISBN 9780310362623 (trade paperback) | ISBN 9780310362630 (ebook)
Subjects: LCSH: Empty nesters. | Middle age—Family relationships. | Separation (Psychology)
Classification: LCC HQ1059.4 .B875 2022 (print) | LCC HQ1059.4 (ebook) | DDC 646.70084/4—dc23/eng/20220121
LC record available at https://lccn.loc.gov/2021041557
LC ebook record available at https://lccn.loc.gov/2021041558

Cover design: Faceout Studio
Cover photo: Kristi Blokhin / Shutterstock
Interior design: Denise Froehlich

Printed in the United States of America

22 23 24 25 26 /LSC/ 10 9 8 7 6 5 4 3 2 1

To Terry and Sharon Hartshorn

You have taught us so very much about living in the empty nest with generosity, commitment, devotion to family, fun, and faith. Thank you!

CONTENTS

FOREWORD

Having kids close together in age was great . . . until they all left at nearly the same time. Honestly, I saw it coming. I anticipated it. And yet, when it really happened, it was a little bit shocking. It was quiet. *So* quiet.

Speaking of quiet, I'll never forget driving back to Georgia after dropping Allie, our youngest, off at Auburn University. It wasn't our first rodeo with college drop-off, but it meant everyone was *really* gone. It was a quiet ride home. I think Andy was afraid to talk. Like, he might say the wrong thing. So he chose silence. It was a good choice. When he asked if I needed a Chick-fil-A ice-cream cone, I was able to squeak out a yes, but that was all I had.

It didn't take long, though, to realize there were some pretty sweet perks to the empty nest. I wasn't making lunches early in the morning. Instead, I was sipping coffee in my quiet-time chair—Bible in my lap and Allie's dog wedged in the chair with me. The dog is mine now. Perk!

I began to realize there were so many things I was excited about doing. I had been super intentional about saying "not right now" to opportunities while the kids were home. Now I could consider saying yes. I said yes to getting my master's degree from Dallas Theological Seminary. It was an amazing experience. Sidenote: I found that I took my studies *way* more seriously than I did with my undergrad degree. Perk!

I upped my speaking and writing yeses, especially as they revolved around foster kids and foster parenting, which had been a big part of our journey once our kids were teenagers. Perk!

Andy and I were having a ball with some speaking together and traveling a little bit. We picked up some new hobbies, and we started working out together instead of separately. Perk!

I'm guessing you're holding this book because you're standing on the precipice of a new and unfamiliar season too. Maybe you're in it already and trying to sort out your emotions and next steps. Or maybe, like us, you're going through this material with your small group. Either way, it's a tricky transition moving into the empty-nester years.

I'd like to share one of my all-time-favorite verses of Scripture. It falls right smack in the middle of a pretty famous psalm of David's. Psalm 139 speaks of God's extraordinary awareness of you. He sees you. He knows you. And there is never any point in trying to hide from his sight. From there David continues by highlighting God's intimate involvement in knitting you together and creating you uniquely and wonderfully.

But here's my favorite part: "All the days ordained for me were written in your book before one of them came to be." Not only did he make you, he knows every single one of your days, and he's known them always. Even the empty-nester ones. How cool is that?

Fast-forward to the New Testament. The writer of the book of Hebrews uses the metaphor of a race: "And let us run with perseverance the race marked out for us" (Heb. 12:2). God has a plan, a race, for you. Even in this next season of life.

I am so excited about *Finding Joy in the Empty Nest* by Jim Burns. Andy and I have learned so much from Jim over the years. Most recently, our small group spent six Monday nights learning how to find the right rhythm in our parenting of full-on adult kids with his book *Doing Life with Your Adult Children*.

In *Finding Joy in the Empty Nest*, Jim nails it again. He harnesses research and lots of stories that offer insight and wisdom in navigating what can certainly be a challenging transition. As you dive into the book, you'll be confronted with ten principles that will propel you to a fresh start and renewed vision. You'll laugh. You'll be inspired. And you'll be motivated to run the race God has marked out for *you*. The one he's known about from the beginning of time.

—Sandra Stanley

ACKNOWLEDGMENTS

Cathy: You have made our life together beautiful in every stage of our marriage.

Christy, Rebecca, Heidi, Steve, Andy, Matt, James, Charlotte, and Huxley: We are family, and I could not be more blessed!

Cindy Ward: So grateful for your partnership in our mission and for all you do every day to make HomeWord such a remarkable organization.

Randy Bramel, Ned Brines, Rod Emery, DeAnn Carroll, Patrick Daniels, Todd Dean, Doug Fields, Bob Howard, Tracy Kuntz, David Lane, Tom Purcell, Theresa Sinclair, and Ken Verheyen: There has never been a better board of directors to work with as we go about helping families succeed. Thank you.

Seth Bartlette, Rodney Bissell, Courtnay Brown, Chris Cannon, Doug Fields, Lynn Juliusson, Shawn King, Jim Liebelt, Roger Marsh, Deb Pflieger, Lori Sargent, Doug Webster, Janelle Webster, and Cindy Ward: I can't believe I get to work with such talented and gifted people. So grateful.

Greg Johnson: World's best literary agent and a dear friend.

Mick Silva: You make editing fun. Thank you for making this a better book and entertaining me with your comments.

Randy and Susan Bramel: Once again, it's your fault I wrote this book. Thank you for your friendship, support, and mentorship.

Randy Bramel, Tom Purcell, Rod Emery, and Terry Hartshorn: How did I become so fortunate to get to meet with you every Tuesday morning? Deeply grateful.

INTRODUCTION

Get Ready for Something New

On the drive home from dropping our youngest daughter off at college, my wife and I both went silent for about two hours. Periodically, I looked over at Cathy, and more than a few times, I watched a tear take a stroll down her cheek. If someone had been watching us, they would have thought that instead of experiencing a beautiful transitional moment in our family's life, we were mourning the death of a loved one. When we arrived home, the house that had been headquarters to constant action, no little amount of tension through the teen years, noise, movement, chaos, laughter, memories, traditions, and more noise was tomblike quiet. We had just entered the empty nest, and not only were we unprepared, but we had been so busy with life that we hadn't even seen it coming.

The following night, I sat down to dinner. Cathy had prepared a massive amount of food. She said, "I guess I need to adjust my cooking portions." As I performed my nightly kitchen-cleanup duty, I put more food back into the refrigerator than we had eaten. Yes, we were going to have to make some adjustments, and we later realized it wasn't just in meal planning but in practically every aspect of our lives. After all, we had just devoted twenty-three years to the daily parenting of our children, who had now morphed into adults (sort of), and we were no longer needed on a day-to-day basis. In addition, we had buried a few of our marriage issues under the "taking care of the kids mat," and we had some work to do.

Just about the time we were getting used to the empty nest, our adult children started moving back home, and we had to learn how to do life with boomerang children. All three of our girls came back through our revolving door several times. Authorities tell us that the average age to begin empty nesting is 48.7 years. We think our last boomerang happened a few months ago, when we were sixty-seven. But hey, isn't sixty the new forty?

No doubt the transition to the empty nest was harder on Cathy. I had my work and was overly focused on it. Cathy was still working as a teacher, but in our home, she had been the sun and we were all her planets. She was a bit lost without her leadership role. (I think she was depressed for a while, but a husband's diagnosis should sometimes go unmentioned.) We later learned she was experiencing what is called the empty-nest syndrome.

As a bit of foreshadowing, I'll share an observation

from Heidi, our youngest, when she was about five years old. Trying to figure out the pecking order of our family, she asked, "Dad, if Rebecca [middle child] bosses me and Christy [our oldest] is the boss of Rebecca, and Mom is the boss of everybody, then are you the boss of anyone?"

But Cathy wasn't the only one who discovered she needed to reinvent herself. I had some work to do in that department myself.

For many people, the empty nest brings other issues to the forefront, such as being caught in the middle of caring for aging parents, caring for needy adult children, health issues, menopause, and changing roles in marriage. Sometimes in-law issues get complicated, as do the problems of finances and future retirement. The list can quickly become a long one. Our road undoubtedly will be full of twists and turns and some unexpected thorns, but even with all that life naturally throws at us, I'm convinced that if you take just a little time to prepare, the empty-nest years can be your best years.

Many individuals spend more time in the empty nest than with their children in the home. Whether you are single, married, or in a blended family, the empty nest brings both the joy of victory and the agony of some defeat. You have to cope with loss and find your new identity. You make midlife course corrections. If you are married, you once again gaze into each other's eyes as you did before you had kids, though those eyes may have more wrinkles and your faces may be fuller than they were two decades ago. Unless you did an amazing job preparing for the empty nest, and most of us didn't, you may be looking at a stranger who is going through their own identity crisis.

I've spent my entire adult life researching, speaking on, and writing about the values of strong marriages, confident parents, and empowered kids. Yet the empty nest took me by surprise. It was much more difficult than I'd thought it would be—and if this makes any sense, much better too. I've told friends that I wrote this book out of my need (desperation?) to reinvent and recalibrate parts of my life, my marriage, and even my relationships with my adult children. Very quickly, the research for this book became personal because I found myself reading for my own benefit before I could write or speak one sentence to others. To be candid, some of the writing on this subject seemed a bit trite, even shallow. "Plant a garden, join a bridge club, and volunteer at the hospital." These are great ideas, but as I listened to the people around me, I learned that empty nesting is more about a sense of loss and the need to find new purpose and passion, while changing the relationships we once had with our children.

It's possible that your best years are ahead of you, and how you choose to live will determine the outcome. I believe that most games are won in the second half and that you, no doubt, have a beautiful though possibly not easy road ahead of you. It's odd for me to give a brief illustration about good wine since I don't drink, but it's a fact that the aging of wine improves its quality. Sometimes an aged wine is dramatically better and more distinguished because it is stored with care. As we age, we can learn from our experiences and improve our lives to finish well. It's my prayer that this book will help you do that.

I've kept this quote from the Old Testament close to my heart: "Be alert, be present. I'm about to do something brand-new. It's bursting out! Don't you see it? There it is! I'm making a road through the desert, rivers in the badlands" (Isa. 43:19 MSG).

As you launch your kids into the world, be alert, present, and prepared: you're launching yourself as well. I hope you will make empty nesting a meaningful, rich, and even fun time amid struggle, perhaps a few tears, and grief. Your children are not who they once were. And neither are you.

Let's get to know who that new person is.

Chapter 1

EMPTY OR FULL? CHALLENGE
OR OPPORTUNITY?

Principle 1: When your child leaves home and their life fills up with fresh experiences, follow their lead.

"I miss their mess. I miss their noise. I miss their rudeness and neediness. I miss their laughter. I miss my place in their lives. Who am I, and what do I do with the rest of my life?"

How does the empty nest feel? You will get different answers from each person you ask. But one of the main reactions people have is usually one level deeper than their first answer. "It's really, really quiet." Let's face it. From the moment you have a baby until the time you launch that child into adult-hood, life is often busy and full of needs to meet. If you are like most parents, you put part of your life on the back burner for more than twenty years. Your world revolves around the kids' schedules, the kids' demands, and even the kids' chaos. Then one day, much of it is gone. The kids are eager to leave home and begin their lives as adults. Your house, and yes, even your life, feels, well, sort of empty. One mom we know said, "I survived twenty-three years of 'forced labor.' Now that I have control of my schedule after all these years, I have no idea what to do with myself." During those days of hectic schedules, we yearn for quiet, but when it abruptly appears, the quiet can really mess with us.

Cathy and I live exactly a half mile from our high-school football stadium. For nine years, this is where we spent our Friday nights in the fall. If the team had an away game, we drove to another stadium. You'd think that as parents of all girls, football would not be part of our lives, but all three girls were cheerleaders. So we faithfully climbed the stands to sit in the "cheer section" and watch the games. We were used to watching a lot of sports because the girls had been junior-high cheerleaders as well as competitive cheerleaders on a travel team. Nothing like driving a vanload of teenage girls from Orange County, California, to Las Vegas for three days so they can perform their 2.45-minute routine twice.

I remember the moment it all stopped. It was the first

Friday night after we had taken our youngest to college. Cathy and I were sitting at the kitchen table. Suddenly, we heard the band playing and the announcer welcoming the cheering fans to the first football game of the year. We looked at each other and wondered whether we should go watch the last half. We didn't go to the game. The overwhelming atmosphere was that of a really quiet house. Our feelings and thoughts were all over the place. We felt a bit of aimlessness, mixed with purposelessness and maybe some restlessness. At the same time, in that quietness, we felt an underlying dose of excitement and wonder. Just as our kids were going through their own rites of passage, so were we.

Change and Loss Are Deeply Connected

Experts say that as your life changes and your kids move out of the house, you can experience an overwhelming sense of loss. Change and loss are deeply connected. Sometimes loss is as simple as that depicted in a cartoon I saw recently. It showed a mom and dad waving goodbye to their young adult child who is moving away from home. The husband turns to his wife, who is crying, and says, "Don't cry, honey. We will find other tech support." Yet many people feel a much deeper sense of loss, like the woman who told me, "The adjustment of not being a part of my kid's day-to-day life hit me like a ton of bricks. I felt emotional pain and a loss of purpose." I think she sums up the feelings of many parents once their kids are given the passport to adulthood. The kids appear to be doing fine, but the parents are grieving the loss. The people who cope best with the empty nest are those who are willing to recognize their grief. It's possible that this period in your life will bring to the surface loneliness, doubt, and worry about the future. I remember staring at Cathy in silence one evening in our now-noiseless home. I was excited that we could spend more time together but also frightened that we had some work to do in our relationship. Our kids had been our major distraction, our excuse for a lack of connection. Would we have anything to say to each other?

When I wrote the book *Doing Life with Your Adult Children*, I didn't realize I had hit on such a critical topic for parents with adult kids. The book kept selling and the stories kept mounting. One of the key issues I chose not to write about in that book is the empty nest. Yet since the book's publication, the topic has consistently surfaced in conversations and questions at every seminar, talk, or webinar I've given. It typically appears when discussing change and loss. So I began to research life after the kids move out. The phrase *empty-nest syndrome* showed up everywhere.

The interesting fact about this syndrome is that it's not a clinical diagnosis or a mental disorder but rather a feeling, an emotion, a mood, and even a burden. One woman put it this way: "I was terrified. I had no idea what I was going to do now that I was no longer anchored by school runs and filling the refrigerator. When I looked at my life minus my children in the house, it looked dark and gloomy. I dreaded it. My existence seemed almost meaningless, like part of me had died."

The Empty-Nest Syndrome

Parents experience normal feelings of sadness, loss, angst, and loneliness when their children leave home. It's normal, but not necessarily anticipated. Some experience deep pain like the man who told me, "When my son left home, I was distraught. I felt like I had lost part of myself. I felt gutted." In a televised interview, rock singer and pop-culture icon Madonna confided that sending her daughter off to the University of Michigan was "an absolutely devastating experience" that sent her reeling "into the deepest depression."[1] For other parents, it's not as intense, even though they still need to create a healthy transition into this new phase of their lives. Unfortunately, the empty nest sometimes coincides with other changes mentioned previously, such as the onset of menopause, the breakdown of the marriage, dealing with an illness or the loss of parents, divorce, moving, retirement, financial stress, and adult children violating the family's values.

Since the empty-nest syndrome usually sneaks up on us, I created the Empty-Nest Syndrome Quiz to help you identify how you're doing.

The Empty-Nest Syndrome Quiz

On a scale of one to five, with five being the highest level
of intensity, mark the intensity of your feelings.

I have experienced a sense of loss in the empty nest.

1	2	3	4	5

I have had trouble adjusting to the
change in my parental role.

1	2	3	4	5

I have experienced a lack of purpose
in life since my kids left.

1	2	3	4	5

I often feel deeply alone.

1	2	3	4	5

I have felt a loss of interest or energy in my love life.

1	2	3	4	5

I have felt depressed or anxious more often.

1	2	3	4	5

I have noticed a loss of self-identity since the children left.

1	2	3	4	5

I sometimes feel like the best years are behind me.

1	2	3	4	5

Empty or Full? Challenge or Opportunity?

I have a lot of fear about the future.

1	2	3	4	5

I am too often preoccupied with my absent
children's safety and welfare.

1	2	3	4	5

Score

40–50 Full alert! But don't despair just yet. It's gonna be okay.

30–40 Intense feelings have brought you here. Read on.

20–30 Okay, average level of freaking out. Not too bad.

10–20 Good for you. Maybe you should be writing this book.

0–10 Hmm. That doesn't seem right. Are you sure?

How you perform on this self-grading quiz doesn't indicate whether you pass or fail at living in the empty nest. It's more of a self-awareness experience to see how much effort it will require to put your life in order and make your empty-nest years the best. Remember, part of your life moved out of the house. Now it's time to reinvent your life and not only thrive but have a different and better relationship with your adult kids. I like how American humorist Erma Bombeck puts it: "When mothers talk about depression of the empty nest, they're not mourning the passing of all those towels on the floor, or the music that numbs your teeth, or the bottle of capless shampoo dribbling down the shower drain. They're upset because they have gone from supervisor of a child's life to spectator. It's like being the vice president of the United States." Yes, moving from supervisor to spectator is tough, but it also can give you freedom to reinvent yourself for the better. So now is the time to take some of that quiet space and recalibrate your life for the better.

That is not to say that raising kids is not great. There is no better investment of your time and energy. It's just that in this new empty-nest season, it is time for you to step out and do whatever it takes to create a second-half experience that is wonderful for your family and for you. To make a healthy transition and move forward with passion and purpose, we must ask the big question: "Now what?"

Now What?

Too many people get stuck living in the past, believing that their best years are behind them when that does not have to be the case. No matter what your age or experience, almost all games are won in the second half, and you can think of the empty nest as your second half. The opportunities before you are limitless. There is no better time to start than right now. Dr. Margaret Rutherford says it best: "Your child's life is filled with fresh experiences. It's good if yours is as well."

Sometimes all we need is a fresh start and a new perspective to move us forward. Following are stories of two different families who dealt with the empty nest in a positive way. What strikes me about both stories is that they found fresh experiences with simplicity.

Patricia and Toby: Reboot and Reconnect

Patricia told me that having her youngest leave home was one of the most difficult experiences of her life. She had never heard of the empty-nest syndrome before hearing me speak on it, but when I explained it, she said, "Yes, that was me in every way." I could tell she was not wallowing in her fears and believed her best years were ahead of her. I asked her what she did to find her way. Patricia was an accountant who gave up the sixty-hour work-week grind as children came along. She worked twenty hours a week at home, adapting her life to the lives of the children. Toby didn't feel the pain of the empty nest as much as Patricia did. He had his work and routines. On the other hand, Patricia felt like her entire life needed a reboot, and she desperately wanted to reconnect with Toby. Out of those quiet moments at home, Pat and Toby worked together to create a simple plan to reboot and reconnect for the first six months. Here was their list:

- Clean out and declutter the closets.
- Join a women's group at church.

- Commit to a weekly date night.
- Join a gym.
- Redo the backyard garden.
- Connect regularly with the kids and visit them monthly.

Even though none of these new experiences was dramatic, they did help Toby and Patricia enter their new phase of life. Cleaning out the closets was therapeutic for Patricia. Her new involvement with a women's group helped her find deeper community with some replenishing relationships. The weekly date night was rejuvenating Toby and Pat's connection while bringing some much-needed fun into their relationship. The backyard garden became a six-month process that again brought the two of them together on a project, although Patricia told me with a twinkle in her eye that she did 80 percent of the work. Toby found that regular gym workouts reduced his stress and helped him lose some weight. And of course, they kept up with the kids and lived close enough to visit at least monthly. Sometimes answers are found in the simple adjustments and baby steps we can all make.

Isabella: Try New Things

You would love Isabella. She is a single mom who told me she cried every time she opened her younger daughter's closet after she left home. She said that for the first week, she mostly sat on the couch after work and ate everything in sight. She cuddled with her dog and wondered whether this was going to be her life for the rest of her days. Yet after facing some of her fears, she knew she had to try new things and make a habit of them. Here was her list:

- Plan new activities.
- Make new friends.
- Plan a trip to New York City for retail therapy with her younger daughter.
- Have weekly Sunday-night appetizers with her married daughter and son-in-law, who lived nearby.
- Deal with a few ghosts from her past that she had not dealt with because of the busyness of life, work, and her daughters.

Again, it was in simplicity that Isabella found her new normal. She told me with a smile that in the later teen years, her younger daughter had been "part best friend, part enemy." They had spent a lot of time together. Isabella had never lived alone, and now that her daughter was out of the house, it was going to be a rough adjustment. She laughed and confessed one of her worries: "Who is going to hold me accountable to not eat half a gallon of ice cream at a time?" She needed to plan new activities.

She signed up for a Pilates class that met three times a week and asked one of her friends from work to join her at church on Sundays. She went out of her way to meet new people and reconnected with others she knew but hadn't spent any time with for a long while. One of her smartest moves to keep connected with her younger daughter was planning a weekend with her in New York City, about a four-hour drive away. She rented an Airbnb for the special weekend, and they planned to do some "retail therapy" for connection.

Her weekly Sunday-evening appetizer time with her older daughter and son-in-law was also a great way to stay grounded and connected. She says her relationship with them has become more peer-like. She claims that has been a game changer. And for Isabella, the biggest game changer was that she started going to counseling about her past abusive relationship and found healing for the "ghosts of her past."

A Fresh Start Begins with You

Somewhere in the silence, we must answer questions: "Who am I? What do I do with the rest of my life?" The stories of Isabella and Patricia and Toby aren't your stories, but they do speak of creating a fresh start. The people I meet who are thriving in the empty nest don't just wait for life to happen. They choose to see new possibilities. They are reinventing their lives, or at least part of their lives. It's an adventure, and it takes some courage to step out of your comfort zone, but most tell me it has been totally worth it.

The people who thrive in their second half and overcome the empty-nest syndrome have taken some important steps toward a fresh start. Here is what I observe they did to make it happen:

1. **They closed the chapter.** It can be difficult to create a new starting point when you haven't had a proper ending. It means realizing that you must build relationships with your adult children on a different level than before. It means accepting the fact that life is going to be different, but it doesn't have to be bad. It means properly closing one chapter to open the next.

2. **They chose to change their attitude.** It's difficult to create a clean beginning if you are feeling too negative about the future. These people found an excitement about new possibilities and adventures that would enhance their second half. With this excitement came positivity toward the future. I've always loved this quote by pastor Chuck Swindoll: "The remarkable thing is we have a choice every day regarding the attitude we embrace for that day. We cannot change our past. . . . We cannot change the fact that people will

act in a certain way. We cannot change the inevitable. The only thing we can do is play the one string we have, and that is our attitude. . . . I am convinced that life is 10 percent what happens to me and 90 percent how I react to it."[2]

3. **They set new goals.** Those goals could be as simple as signing up for a gym membership or as challenging as changing careers. Developing new goals brings a sharp focus on a new purpose. There is no doubt that the empty nest gives you an opportunity to declutter your life. It could be a closet or a garage, or it could be some old ways of living. You have more time with the kids out of the house, but how will you invest it? Create some goals that can help you thrive in the empty nest, and remember that many of the people who do well added goals for finding a deeper spiritual connection.

4. **They made new friends and enhanced their old friendships.** People who thrived in the empty nest learned that they measured happiness by how deeply connected they were to others. In the second half of life, spending quality time with friends and loved ones is one of the key areas of happiness as well as of living a meaningful life. For some people, it means taking more chances and putting themselves in new situations.

Empty or Full? Challenge or Opportunity?

Over the last couple of years, I have asked hundreds of people in focus groups and at conferences to talk with me about the empty nest. I talked to singles, couples, those just beginning to prepare for the empty nest, and those old enough to have adult kids ready to launch their own children into adulthood. I didn't come to those times ready to speak or teach. I came with pen and paper in hand, ready to listen and learn. (I know, pen and paper are a little old-fashioned, but that's how I roll.) Those times were amazing and so informative. Later as I started speaking on the subject, I realized that the empty nest was a major concern for those in the second half of life. If you are an empty nester, you probably remember Jim McKay, the voice of *ABC's Wide World of Sports*. He passed away several years ago, but few will ever forget the music at the beginning of that show and his voiceover narrative about "the thrill of victory and the agony of defeat." That phrase describes how I felt about my conversations with empty nesters.

Most of the focus groups featured tears. And usually laughter. Some couples were tense, and some looked like they were on their second honeymoon. I met single moms and a few single dads who had special stories to tell. It reminded me that the empty nest isn't just about couples. Almost all the people said that, yes, they had experienced, to some extent, the empty-nest syndrome, and for many it was quite severe. Generally, women struggled more than men. But after hundreds of hours of listening, learning, and reading everything I could on the subject, and reflecting on my own experience, I came up with several key principles for thriving in the second half of life. I want to introduce you to those life-changing principles in the rest of this book.

When you enter the empty nest, you may feel too tired to rebuild or create new opportunities. I get it. You just ran a twenty-year marathon, and most likely there was very little, if any, celebration at the end of it. Most people experience the gamut of feelings. They are often torn between wanting their kids to stay home and wanting to help them launch their new lives as adults. It seems like just when you are getting into the groove of this parenting thing, it all changes. But in the stillness, in those quiet moments, you'll find answers for your second half.

Don't be afraid of the stillness. That's where you will find the strength to thrive and to reinvent what needs to be reinvented.

Chapter 2

REINVENTING THE RELATIONSHIP WITH YOUR ADULT CHILDREN

Principle 2: Always keep responsible adulthood in mind as the goal. And remember, experience is a better teacher than your advice.

"It's really not about you anymore. As he makes the shift to adulthood, he won't need to see you as much as you want to see him."

Mary and Mike sit at the kitchen table most every morning drinking coffee, skimming the news, and talking. Sounds to me like a great start to a day in the empty nest, except Mike tells me that most of that time and energy is negative.

"Mary just keeps fussing, fuming, and worrying about our four adult kids, two grandchildren, and two daughters-in-law," he confides.

"But isn't one of your kids doing well in a ministry position?" I ask. "And isn't it looking like your son is on his way to making the Olympic volleyball team?"

"It doesn't matter," Mike tells me. "She is worried about their lifestyle choices, faith differences, political leanings, and just about everything else. She thinks they drink too much, and she is worried about how the two grandkids are being parented."

He says with exasperation, "It starts in the morning, and it's often how we spend our evenings. This is just not how I envisioned our time together in the empty nest."

"Are her concerns valid?" I ask.

He thinks for a moment and says, "Sure. We didn't imagine some of the silly decisions our kids would make. We didn't raise them this way."

Mary is mostly right, but it's causing her to be stuck, unfocused and unprepared to move forward with her life. On the other hand, Mike is charging full speed ahead with his career. He has just become a vice president at his company and has been asked to join the leadership team at his church. Mike brings out a very worn copy of my book *Doing*

Life with Your Adult Children.[3] He says, "We've both read the book and have even been through the course. Mary believes your principles are very important, but she obviously isn't following them."

Like most of us, Mary and Mike have some work to do if they want to thrive in their second half. Reinventing your relationship with your adult children is a process. No one can expect their adult kids to instantly act like adults, and parents of adult children must go through the process of accepting that their role has changed forever. But the good news is that it can be reinvented into something positive and healthy. Most likely it's going to take some work, perseverance, and a willingness to adapt. You undoubtedly will need to change your expectations to match the new reality—a lot.

What's a Parent to Do?

According to my research and my personal experience, the parents who do the best with the empty nest acknowledge that part of their lives has moved out of the house. From that day forth, they are a bit separated from their children, and frankly, as harsh as it may sound, that's the way it's supposed to be. Even if we prepare for being less needed, it's often a huge adjustment to accept that we are no longer their cornerstones, their anchors, the fixers of meals, the keepers of schedules. We are no longer in control. One mom told me,

"I had to acknowledge the roller coaster of emotions I was having after a twenty-year vocation where I had been focused on anything from wiping noses to staying up late with my kids. Suddenly, I was fired and not needed as much."

You first have to adjust to the reality of not being a part of your child's day-to-day life. If you are grieving that loss, recognize it and accept that it will take time before you can refocus your life. In the best of relationships, you are moving from mom to mom-mentor, dad to dad-advisor. The best relationships with adult children eventually become more peer-like. You will always be their parent, but you move from a parent-child relationship to a parent-adult relationship. The goal is always the same: your children's responsible adulthood. You'll just have less direct influence on that going forward.

Our family went on an incredible beach trip together after Christmas. Every day, we had hours of hanging out and playing on the beach. It was truly a great connection time. But more than that, when Cathy and I debriefed the trip, we realized that we had finally experienced a rite of passage for our family. Our kids had become responsible adults, and we enjoyed their company. Sure, they live a bit differently than we do. They believe things that we don't believe. They experience life in their own way. But our job is to love them, enjoy them, and support them with encouragement while recognizing that we are no longer responsible for their behavior. I like what advice columnist Ann Landers wrote years ago: "It is not what you do for your children but what you have taught them to do for themselves that will make them successful human beings."

The transition wasn't easy for Cathy and me, and I'm not sure it was even that easy for our kids. Here are five big questions that were helpful to us that might help you reinvent your relationship with your adult children.

The Five Big Questions

1. Have you given your child the passport to adulthood? Letting go of a mindset is seldom easy. Everything inside us as parents with good motives wants to hold on and be in charge. But we must reinvent the relationship by giving our children the passport to adulthood, even if they aren't behaving like adults. I believe it is the parents' job to take the lead and rewrite the script by letting go. (I didn't say this would be easy.) It is our job to acknowledge that we are no longer in charge. We must recognize that our priorities are not always going to be their priorities. They are not going to communicate with us the way we want them to or as frequently as we'd like. The quicker you acknowledge a loss of control, the quicker you have a shot at moving your relationship to an adult-to-adult connection.

Janet panicked when her son, who was at college two

thousand miles away, got serious with a girlfriend from his university and announced he wasn't moving home after graduation. She told her husband to find him a job in their county and that if her son was serious with this girl, she could move to their community. The young woman had a good job offer in the town she was living in, and her son loved that same area, which was where he had gone to school. Janet's husband was torn trying to help Janet through a mounting depression and maintaining the relationship with his son, who wasn't going to move home. I get it. Having kids living a long distance or even a short distance away is tough, but they are now in charge, and you are not. Another mom we know realized she was transitioning to life with an empty nest and offered to pay her son to move back into the house. Not a good idea.

I remember the day our daughter Becca came home from college a few months into her freshman year with a hoop nose ring. As a parenting communicator, I've always said, "Choose your battles," and that nose rings and tattoos are not on my list of battles. But now it was *my* daughter wearing *that* nose ring, and before I could compose myself, she saw my smirk, which silently said, "You've got to be kidding me!"

She looked at me and with a similar smirk (is smirking an inherited trait?) just said, "Whaat?"

I said, "Nothing, why?" (Okay, I lied just a bit.)

She was a bit healthier about it than me. "My nose ring?"

She pointed to the hoop. It wasn't very large, but in my mind, it took up half her face.

I quickly regrouped and ended up saying, "Your nose, your decision."

Later, I wondered what kind of message she was trying to relay. I think it was something like this: "I'm in charge now, and I want to wear a nose ring. But also, can you still pay my car insurance and cell phone bill?" Much deeper than that was, "If I live differently than you would have done in college and adulthood, will you still love me?"

It is up to parents to answer that question with their words and actions. Your disagreements may be about different things, but you will have some. Let them make their own image and lifestyle choices.

By the way, fifteen years later, Becca still wears the nose ring. And now I think it's cute.

2. Are you enabling dependency? No one seeks to enable dependency with their adult children. Well, maybe a few people do, but most of us want to help our kids without enabling them. Unfortunately, no one sent us to adult-child parenting school, and we sometimes get it wrong. If you are a helicopter parent, land the helicopter. If you are still making appointments for your adult children, stop it. I know they might not get to the dentist as quickly as you would like, but if the bottom line is developing responsible adults, then it's time for them to learn to act like one and make their appointments (and do hundreds of other things) on their own. Enabling dependency most often equals a failure to launch, and that is not what we want.

One family I know allowed their daughter to continue using the family credit card even after she was married. They complained that their newlywed daughter and her husband were not being responsible with their finances, but the problem was not with the daughter. It was with the parents, who kept the money tree happening. I don't have a problem if parents help responsible adult children with finances for a good reason. About 75 percent of parents help their children financially at one time or another, but ongoing bill paying is not healthy. Remember the high cost of money on relationships, and don't make it complicated. We too often make things worse by not communicating clearly or not defining expectations. Most often, whether it is with money or another issue, saying I love you means saying no to enabling.

If I asked one hundred parents of adult children whether they believe experience is a better teacher than advice, at least ninety-nine of them would agree. Yet we often want to ease pain for our kids. But hear me: this is not allowing them to experience failure. And without that? Management guru Peter Drucker says it this way: "Nobody learns except by making mistakes."[4] Drucker was speaking about business management, but it's some of the best parenting advice too.

Allow your kids to make mistakes. We do them no favors if we are always bailing them out of learning experiences.

I love this dialogue between two parents: "But how are we supposed to make sure that she actually does her work if we don't know her grades on a weekly basis?"

"I don't think you are supposed to make sure she gets her work done. Isn't that up to her?"

Again, no one said this would be easy. Remember the African proverb "They will never know how far the town is if you carry them on your back."

Practicing a form of tough love doesn't involve offering retribution for poor choices. It means showing love and positivity to your kids while allowing them to experience the consequences of their choices. Early in our daughters' adult years, we saw them making decisions that didn't please us. Their decisions weren't life or death. They simply were not what we would do or want them to do. During those years, I came up with a phrase that helped me: "Does it really matter?" If you take some time to think through the most and least likely scenarios, you'll find that some things do matter, but most things do not. And remember that poor choices can result in growth and understanding. For them to launch successfully, it's going to take major doses of discipline on your part. If you are their biggest cheerleader and support them emotionally and spiritually, then when they crash, they will look to you for mentoring and advice.

3. Do you want it more than they want it? It happens every time I speak on doing life with adult children. A person will come up to me at the end and share a story of their child's violating their values as a parent. The parent is heartbroken, and usually for good reason. Parents usually feel more pain than their children do.

Gerald and Alexa are a wonderful ministry couple with five kids. I know them personally, and they are great parents. One of their daughters moved cross-country to attend college. About five months into the academic year, they found a social media account that revealed their daughter had become quite the party girl. She had moved out of the dorm and was living with her boyfriend. She was rejecting the values taught at home, rejecting the faith lived out at home, and living her way.

Yes, great parents can still have adult children who make poor choices. Gerald and Alexa were stunned. Their first thought was to fly out, pick up their daughter, and bring her home. Another thought, which came from deep within their hurt mixed with anger, was to shun her. Remove the privileges and reject her.

They chose a better way.

They did fly out to see her. In love, they confronted her about her decisions. From the beginning, they told her that they loved her and that since she was an adult, she would have to make some decisions. They said they felt it was their responsibility to remind her what they believed about her actions and how they felt. They also reminded her that there were consequences to her decisions. Since she was making "adult decisions" like living with her boyfriend while they were paying for an empty dorm room, they were going to stop paying for her education. They agreed to pay for her flight home at Christmas and would continue to send care packages, basically reminding her that the relationship was going to be strong and loving. But there would be natural consequences for her "my life, my choices" lifestyle.

They reported back to me that the conversation had not gone as well as they had hoped. She was angry at their decision not to pay for school. She confronted them for being unloving, even saying something like, "And you call yourselves Christians!" They held their ground and flew home devastated.

They knew in their hearts that they weren't defined by their child's poor choices, but they were still grieving and doubting what had happened. They were caught in the messy middle of wanting to show love but being firm about the unwise and unhealthy decisions their daughter made. They knew they couldn't want it more than she wanted it. And they knew they needed to forgive their daughter for some of her poor choices, which they both said was difficult for them.

Speaking of forgiveness, when our kids choose to color outside our moral lines or choose a life different from ours, it is healthy to forgive. I think it is possible to forgive and not act judgmental, while still disagreeing with them. A lack of forgiveness erects a major roadblock in the relationship. Writer Anne Lamott's statement is so true on several levels: "Not forgiving is like drinking rat poison and then waiting for the rat to die."[5] Forgiving our children for their poor choices helps us avoid dumping our anger and frustration on them. We need to deal with our pain and exasperation, but it's best not to make our adult children the target of our emotions, even though they are causing our anguish.

As we learn not to want it more than they want it, we must realize that their priorities will not be our priorities, that their values might not be our values, and that we are not defined by our children's choices. Too many parents of adult children who are making poor choices become so concerned about what others will think that they aren't willing to share their hurt with anyone, which is never healthy. One of my favorite sayings is, "We wouldn't be so concerned about what people think of us if we realized how little they do." My advice is to find safe people to talk with through your heartbreak. I like this proverb: "Where there is no guidance, a people falls, but in an abundance of counselors there is safety" (Prov. 11:14 ESV).

Jill Savage, in her excellent book on the empty nest, writes that although you laid a good foundation for your children as they grew up, they still must choose to build their own houses on that foundation. A friend of Jill's once said, "If they decide to build a shack on the foundation you laid for them, your job is to pray they'll eventually tear down the shack and build the beautiful castle you laid the foundation for."[6] That's a great way to look at it.

4. Are you communicating with them on an adult level? As your role with your adult children changes, so should the way you communicate with them. We must let go of our desires and expectations. One of the most helpful phrases for doing life with your adult children is "unsolicited advice is usually taken as criticism." Much of the time, our motives are pure. We just want to help. But what they hear is, "We don't trust you." I've had to bite my tongue, and I have the scars to prove it. I like this tweet from writer Rachel Wolchin: "Maturing is realizing how many things don't require your comment."

Experience is a much better teacher than advice, and undoubtedly it will be the most effective way for your adult child to learn, even if it takes longer than you'd hoped. As your role changes from day-to-day advice-giving parent to more of a mentor-coach parent, you will find some rewarding times. The transition typically doesn't happen if you are constantly giving advice, even if you are correct. Adult-to-adult communication occurs over time, and it becomes a rewarding part of your new relationship.

5. Are you ready for the boomerang? Yep, it is very

possible that just as you are getting adjusted to your empty nest and beginning to enjoy it, your child will move back home. All three of our girls moved back a few times. Our front door turned into a revolving door. There were some great joys and some real hardships when the kids boomeranged. When one of our daughters moved in, I remember Cathy saying something like, "With her back home, unemployed, and with an attitude, it's hard to believe I ever suffered from the empty-nest syndrome."

One single mom I know moved out of a large house to save money. She told me that when her son called and asked if he could crash at the house for a few months, she was thrilled. But after a year, it was turning into more of a burden than a joy. She hadn't taken into consideration that his moving back home might add a lot of tension and stress. She smiled and told me that the teenage years had prepared her to welcome the empty nest, and that after her son moved back in, he reverted to his teen behavior. One report revealed that kids' moving back home causes significant health impacts, especially for mothers: 46 percent report sleeping loss and 40 percent report gaining weight.

When kids move back to the once empty nest, it's important to recognize that it doesn't have to be bad. But you have to plan to make the necessary adjustments. And by the way, if the boomerang is visiting your home, you are not alone. The Pew Research Center reported that for the first time in 130 years, young adults ages eighteen to thirty-four were more likely to be living at home than with a spouse or a roommate in their own households.[7] There could be several reasons why your adult child is moving back home. One might center around a delay in getting married. This generation seems to be getting married much later than earlier generations, waiting until their late twenties or thirties. Money, debt, and job access are other major reasons for the boomerang. When the COVID-19 pandemic began, millions of adult children unexpectedly moved back home. Most parents were not prepared for the changes.

No matter the reason, it's important to create agreements and establish boundaries and expectations. Because they are our children, we often tend to avoid the important discussions before they move in, which can bring on frustration, hurt feelings, and misunderstandings. Following are a couple of ideas to make the boomerang more enjoyable.

1. *Express your expectations.* It's quite possible they left your home as teenagers or at least as very young emerging adults, but now they are coming home as adults. You need to treat them as such and be respectful of their change in status. At the same time, you hope they will act like the adults they are and still be respectful of your new role and your house. No, it's not going to be easy, but with some careful planning and a give-and-take dialogue, it can be easier.

When our daughter Becca moved back into the house,

Cathy and I were semiprepared. Experience is a better teacher, and we had not done as well when our oldest daughter, Christy, had moved in the previous year. We had a short list of expectations and a bucket with a toilet brush to help her with the responsibility of cleaning her own bathroom. We tried to set the expectations to a minimum. We asked for a clean bathroom, two meals a week with us, and texting or calling us if she was going to be out past 11:00 p.m., because whether she liked it or not, we would be waiting up if we didn't know when she was coming home. We also asked that she follow the moral code in our home. We were fortunate this was not a problem for her, but it can be and often is for many families.

Without any planning on our part, I asked her if she had any expectations for us. In my mind this was a one-way conversation, but I was quickly corrected. Becca smiled and after thinking about it for a while rattled off several expectations for us that mostly had to do with our treating her like an adult and not reverting to the teenage years. Developing a short agreement about household expectations, establishing ground rules, and setting some boundaries is always helpful. Negotiation, setting expectations, and compromise are always easier before a child moves in.

If we were doing it all over again today, I probably would have come more prepared to ask for my child's expectations of us even before giving her ours. But I'd want it to be natural and not seem like I was just trying to listen before sharing my own list.

2. *Have an honest discussion about money.* Keep in mind the high cost of money on relationships. Don't make it complicated. Even if you have the money, understand that many times, saying I love you to your adult child means saying no to enabling their lack of financial responsibility. Consider charging a nominal rent. One single mom we know said the extra money helped her greatly. Another couple we know charged a small amount of rent money, and then when their son moved out, they gave all the money back to help him with his housing. When it comes to finances and stewardship, the goal is to foster independence and financial responsibility. You never want to become a money tree. That's why it is always beneficial to develop an exit strategy if you are helping with finances. You are teaching them healthy stewardship at the same time.

My son-in-law is a pilot. I remember when he first went to flight school. He said the landings were a bit wobbly and sometimes a little bumpy. Over the years, landing the plane became second nature. Most of the landings were silky smooth. Sure, occasionally the air gets choppy, and the landing can still be rough, but time and practice make the landings much better. It's the same in your new relationship with your adult children. As you reinvent the relationship from parent-child to adult-adult, you'll encounter some bumps in the road. But when you hand them the passport to adulthood, treating them as adults without offering unsolicited advice or enabling them, they eventually get past the awkward years and become responsible adults. This is especially true if we live by the thought at the beginning of this chapter: "It's really not about you anymore. As he makes the shift to adulthood, he won't need to see you as much as you want to see him."

And if you're like most empty nesters, what really helps with reinventing your relationship with your adult kids is doing a little reinventing yourself. That can make the empty nest so much more enjoyable.

Chapter 3

REINVENTING YOURSELF FOR THE REST OF YOUR LIFE

Principle 3: Celebrate this rite of passage and embrace the positive change.

"It's time to create new habits and new adventures with less clutter."

The people who make a successful transition to the empty nest embrace new habits, form new routines, refresh their goals, and find new purpose: they reinvent or recalibrate their lives. Your entire life might not change, but in the empty nest, you have been given back hours of your day and weeks that were once focused on the kids. Now is the perfect time to make some course corrections. Those who adapt to the change and adjust their mindsets are the ones who thrive in a new relationship with their kids as well as embrace new rituals, routines, and adventures. While some empty nesters get stuck focusing on the past, several considerations can help you move forward with a fresh start and renewed vision.

One of the strongest reasons entering the empty nest hits people so hard is because they did not prepare for this new phase of life, and it bites them. That was Cathy's and my experience. We were living by circumstance and chance. After we had maintained a breathless pace with our kids in the chaos of the teenage years, the silence of the empty nest was forced on us, and we were not ready. The smell of fresh linens, a full refrigerator, the TV remote found where we left it, and even the toilet seat closed didn't seem to give us comfort. Instead, the silence screamed, "What now?!"

What Will Your New Life Look Like?

Certainly you have considered what a major milestone it is for your kids to be launched into adulthood. Well, it's a major milestone for you too. Whether you are ready for it or not, you are making a significant and important pivot in your life. Almost all empty nesters admit to a feeling of loss, but this new season also opens new opportunities for growth and purpose. Emily and Mike are my heroes and examples of doing the pivot well. They dropped their youngest son off at Cal Poly, San Luis Obispo, California. They had always wanted to take a drive up the West Coast from California to the Canadian border. It was a bit more complicated when they were juggling kids' schedules, but now was the perfect time. As they said "goodbye and see you soon" to their youngest, they got into the car and headed north up Highway 1 along the beautiful rocky coast for a two-week vacation. Emily told me that she cried for the first hour. That night after a somewhat quiet dinner, they held each other and grieved the loss of a life that had been their major focus for twenty-four years, from the time their first child was born until that day. Thankfully for them, they had been forewarned by some friends who had already experienced the empty nest that those first days can be rough.

As they drove, hiked, rekindled their romance, and enjoyed the beauty of God's nature, they talked about what their new life would be like without their two children in the home. It wasn't like the kids were going to be that far away, but they acknowledged that things were going to be different. They began to remodel their life. They talked about their dreams for the second half. Mike and Emily were close to the average age people begin the empty nest: 48.9 years old. They figured that with good health, it was possible they could spend more time in the empty-nest years than with kids at home. It was hard to imagine.

A few days into the trip, Mike pulled out his notebook and copied a quote from the Old Testament that seemed appropriate for their new life. It was the same quote that has been important for me as well: "Be alert, be present. I'm about to do something brand-new. It's bursting out! Don't you see it?" (Isa. 43:19 MSG).

That verse became the impetus of a plan to reinvent their lives as individuals and as a couple. For Mike and Emily, this was a new season with lots of wonderful potential. They recognized that they didn't have to be afraid of the emptiness that came as their children were launched into adulthood. It could be a time of growth and evolution for them, even as they watched their own young adults make their way in the world. Something brand new was happening in their lives and they both wanted to be alert and intentional about it. They would have to acknowledge that though life as they had known it would be different in many ways, it would have lots of similarities, which felt good for them. They also understood there was a very good chance the kids would move back in as they took their journey into their own adult years, and that they would move back in as adults and not as teens.

Writing that Scripture verse down in a notebook, Mike and Emily added four phrases underneath it:

- physical health
- emotional wholeness

- relational connection
- spiritual intimacy

As they drove up the coast, they talked about their hopes, dreams, and concerns in those four areas, both individually and as a couple. They told me later it was in the silence and time together that energy for their second half emerged.

Emily told me she had emptied herself by putting so much of her energy into the kids and knew she needed some self-care. She had to work through the fact that focusing on self-care was not selfish but rather quite healthy. She knew she needed to give herself permission for some "me time." She told me, "My kids have been my excuse for putting little energy into exercise, friendships, and church involvement, and for not putting as much energy into my marriage." She joined a gym, lost some weight, and joined a women's Bible study at her church, and she told me that she and Mike together renewed their commitment to a weekly date, which had been put aside in the last few years because of his work schedule and the kids' lives. She was on her way, taking some healthy baby steps.

Mike had a similar experience. He renewed his commitment to eat better and get in shape. He wanted to recalibrate their finances, gain control of his work schedule, and become better organized. While on the trip, he called a friend who was a business coach and made a lunch appointment for when he returned. Mike also took a step toward rekindling his relationship with Emily by taking the lead with date-night ideas. And he decided it was time to dust off the golf bag and enjoy a sport he loved but hadn't taken time for the last several years. Mike told me the trip caused him to realize he had gotten way too serious and had quit having fun. I shared with him one of my favorite quotes from Randall Wallace, the author of *Braveheart:* "It's never too late to have a happy childhood." He smiled and said, "I needed to be reminded of that."

Small Changes Equal Amazing New Outcomes

Notice that Mike and Emily's changes weren't massive. They recognized they had more time to focus on some healthy changes that could be the catalyst for a beneficial transformation. How about you? It's not necessary to take a two-week vacation up the entire West Coast to rewrite the script of your life, although a vacation is never a bad idea. Whether you are married or single, you can start with some healthy decisions to thrive in the empty nest.

Change is not as easy as we think. How many times do people set New Year's resolutions on January 1 and lose all momentum to change by January 15? I know, I'm an expert on setting great goals and then not reaching them. My problem is not having a workable plan or system in place after I write down my goals. My suggestion is not only to write your goals but also to create habits for accomplishing them. I've found that I do better with small changes that eventually produce amazing outcomes.[8] The only other option is not a good one. You can do what many people do: neglect creating a blueprint for the second half. When this happens, we get swallowed up by our lack of attention, and positive change gets put on the back burner.

What Will It Take to Thrive in an Empty Nest?

Rather than getting caught up in the gloom of empty nesting, embrace the freedom to reinvent or recalibrate your life. One woman who was clearly missing her old role as day-to-day mom told me, "My time is much more my own than it was before. I miss the energy of the kids' living at home, but I do enjoy having more time to invest in other things that are meaningful to me. I've been given a gift of more hours in the day to do something different. I'm on a quest to sort out my finances and rethink the home. I've finally quit structuring my life around waiting for a call or a text from one of the kids. I really don't want to be needy to my adult children." She was acknowledging her new phase of life and embracing a new relationship with her family. This phase gives us the opportunity to recalibrate our lives. Don't miss it. A bit of remodeling is better not only for you but also for your kids.

As you embrace the changes you can make in your life and in your relationships with your children, don't procrastinate. Live to the fullest while you have the energy. My friend Randy Bramel always says, "Life is short. Life is uncertain. Make the most of it while you can." Very few times in life are as big of a transition as when your kids leave home. It brings with it new opportunities for growth and change. The question is, What will it take for you to make the needed changes so you can thrive in the empty nest? Chances are you already know the answer. Now it's time to put it into practice. These three suggestions may help:

1. Take the time to declutter. Management expert Peter Drucker once said, "First things first, last things not at all."[9] This is just as true for life as it is for business. Let's face the fact that even with the extra time and focus you now have, if you do nothing with them, your life just fills up with other people's agendas and other stuff. That's simply human nature. A much better model for thriving in this season is to ruthlessly eliminate the stuff and obligations that aren't as important. What do you toss and what do you keep? That's a great question for those overfilled closets and the garage, as well as for your choices.

I'm not exactly a neat freak. It's hard for me to get rid of things. When I was in college, anything I didn't want to toss I just slid under my bed. One day my girlfriend, and now my wife, Cathy, saw some trash leaking from under the bed. She asked me about it, and before I could answer, she started pulling all that stuff out and made a pile of things to toss. It was a good lesson for me because almost everything except the signed New York Yankees' Mickey Mantle baseball card got the boot, and I never missed any of it. It's the same with our lives. It's hard to move forward if we don't do a little decluttering.[10]

What parts of your life do you need to toss so that you can invent a better second half? Like I said, you probably already know. Somewhere in my journey, I learned the SEEYA method of decluttering. You might want to try it. SEEYA is an acronym that reminds me to simplify and ditch old ideas and responsibilities that have dust on them. Here is how SEEYA works:

- **Sucks your energy.** What is sucking your energy that could be tossed? Obviously, some things like responsibilities and people can't be tossed. But perhaps you can create better boundaries or safer systems. It takes courage to create clear and healthy communication with people. Sometimes just a tweak is needed. Other times you need to offload a responsibility that drains you. I know a person who resigned from two board positions of organizations he liked, but the responsibilities had become a drudgery and were taking a toll on other parts of his life.

- **Excessive.** One day my wife came downstairs holding an old baseball hat of mine that was, let's just say, well used. (Okay, it was dirty and had sweat stains on it.) She held up the hat and asked if I really needed seventeen baseball hats stacked on the top shelf of our closet. For some reason she thought it was a bit excessive. It was hard, but it felt good to downsize the inventory to five hats with no stains. What is excessive in your life? I am referring not only to hats and material goods but also to needless tasks and senseless responsibilities. One couple realized that they had almost every streaming subscription available because their kids "needed" them all. They dumped five and saved $150 a month. After a short discussion, one couple retired from two committees for which they no longer needed to invest their time.

- **Emotionally draining.** As you ruthlessly eliminate clutter, you will also eliminate stress. One of the biggest stress areas for most families is the breathless pace in which we live. Stress is emotionally draining. The empty nest should give us more margin and leeway. Now that the kids are gone, we can fill up our lives with more activities and responsibilities, or we can build more margin into our lives. Is there something in your life that is emotionally draining and stress producing that can be eliminated? What's holding you back?

- **You don't love or need.** Again, this doesn't include kids or spouses. I'm talking about something at work or in the home or a commitment to a group. The kids are gone and maybe it's time to retire those things that no longer energize you.

- **Annoying eyesore.** When speaking about decluttering, I've asked parents if they have anything they are holding on to that is an annoying eyesore. I always get a response. Sometimes a couple will argue about what an annoying eyesore is and what a treasure is. The problem is that one person's treasure is another person's eyesore. Take, for example, my collection of old Hawaiian shirts. I might even call them vintage. In Cathy's mind, they are annoying eyesores. Another example is our friends' rusty, rickety swing set in their back yard. I had never thought much about it, but I'm sure it hadn't gotten much use for years since their kids were adults. I noticed recently that the swing set had been replaced by a cool sitting area surrounded by a beautiful tropical garden. I complimented them on the upgrade. I thought their response was classic. "It took us fifteen years to replace that swing set because we thought it would bother the kids. Once they left and we replaced it, the kids asked us why it took so long to trash it."

Part of decluttering our lives is letting go of perceptions or memories we're holding on to. We found that for our kids, not all of our many Burns traditions were meaningful for them, and it was time to dump some old ones and bring in some new.

The SEEYA principle has helped me think about all the clutter I tend to keep around my life. Think of your empty nest as a do-over. It's a chance to trim things out of your life that probably should have been trimmed years before. It means setting new limits and boundaries because less stuff often equals less stress. Less stuff equals more freedom to do what you have been wanting to do. Before you can recalibrate, reinvent, and reset your life, you need to declutter so you can thrive in this new season. Don't skip over this. You simply cannot thrive if you are bringing a heavy load into the next part of your journey.

2. Dream on. Once Cathy and I launched our kids into adulthood and did some decluttering, we put together a dream-on list. It was a fun experience that wasn't a one-time event but an ongoing dialogue. Our dream-on list included travel, financial realignment, slowing the pace a bit, relationship goals, physical ambitions, spiritual purpose, and some changes around the house. From that list and our many conversations, Cathy decided to go back into teaching kids with learning disabilities, which was her passion. She started leading a Bible-study group. Just because she had more time didn't mean she was ready to retire and sit around watching old *Hawaii Five-O* reruns. It was time to try new things. I love to read, but during our intense kid years, I didn't have the margin to read novels purely for enjoyment. As a writer and speaker, I typically read only for research for the next talk or the next writing assignment. I have always loved what C. S. Lewis wrote: "Someday you will be old enough to start reading fairy tales again." I've now read several hundred novels, and yes, some fairy tales, and I view my life as even more rewarding because of my dream-on reading plan. The biggest phrase on our dream-on list after the kids left home was "have an adventure."

What is stopping you from creating your own dream-on list?

Most people in the child-raising years don't have time or energy to dream about the future. The second half is an opportunity to look at new situations, fresh environments, and adventures. One man said, "When the kids left home, I was free to dream again." Writer Frank McCourt had always wanted to write a novel, but life was too busy and distracting during the child-raising years. He began writing at age sixty-five. His book *Angela's Ashes* won both the Pulitzer Prize and the National Book Critics Circle Award. It was made into a movie, and museums were even named after him. Our friend Brenda raised her kids and then took up painting. Today she is an accomplished artist. When I ask others what they have on their dream-on list, I hear of people embracing new habits, dreams, and routines. Here is just a partial list: mentoring moms and couples, traveling, starting a new business, building new relationships, going back to school, turning a hobby into a full-time job, volunteering at the cancer center, taking dance lessons, becoming a missionary. Peter and Gail launched their kids and then learned to speak another language. The possibilities are endless. How about you? What's on your dream-on list?

3. Refill the empty nest, but slowly. When it comes to the empty nest, you will either reinvent yourself or your life will reinvent you. It's a choice we all have to make. The people who do best at thriving and reinventing are aware of the positive benefits of the empty nest. They take advantage of the incredible opportunities to make their second half the best years of their lives. Life is an adventure. But the benefits of being intentional about change, even if it's at a slower pace, far outweigh remaining the same.

Just last night, Cathy and I were sitting on the sofa in our family room, drinking some hot tea. It had been a busy day. I had been in my office all day and she had been watching all three of our grandkids for much of the day. I had come home for a quick lunch that lasted two hours because there were a few balls to throw, a doll to help dress, and an irresistible six-month-old who needed to be held. Cathy sighed and said she was exhausted and needed to take a shower. She said she hadn't gotten anything done all day long. I begged to differ. She had done exactly what we had dreamed of doing in the second half: focusing on the grandkids and helping our busy adult children.

We talked for a while about our middle daughter's engagement and an upcoming trip we were taking to see her in Florida. We talked about a home project that started small but had ended up much more complicated that was finally coming to an end. The conversation moved toward the Bible study that Cathy now leads each week and how much she loves the women. We talked about my desire a few years back to have more serious fun in our lives, declutter my workload, and invest in more writing and speaking. I treasure those quiet moments on the sofa. We didn't take that time when the kids were living in the house, and now we have made the time to reconnect, and it has been good. As we got up from that sofa to put the dog out one more time, say a prayer together, and move toward bed, I realized that life will never be perfect (far from it), but that the adjustments and tweaks were bearing fruit, and our dreams for our second half were coming true. And it was good and worth the effort.

— Positive Benefits of the Empty Nest —

Here is a short list of benefits of the empty nest compiled from our focus groups. Undoubtedly you will be able to add many more to it:

1. You can revive romance.
2. Your kids come back to visit, and you can schedule regular times to connect.
3. It's easier to get a good night's sleep.
4. You have more time, and your time is your own.
5. Your home is cleaner and more well organized.
6. You can create new routines and new rules.
7. You can move forward with things that were on the back burner.
8. You can take more trips.
9. You can make plans without smaller kids in the picture.
10. You can enjoy your grandchildren and then hand them back.
11. You can rediscover an old passion or interest.
12. You can find rest more easily and invigorate your soul.
13. You can spend more time with friends and family.
14. You can spend more time in community involvement.

What would you add?

Chapter 4

YOUR EMPTY-NEST MARRIAGE

Winning in the Second Half

Principle 4: Midlife is about staying in love by falling in love again.

"The kids are gone, the house is quiet, and we're dating again."

Falling in love is easy. Staying in love takes much more energy, commitment, and focus. This investment leads to falling in love again, more meaningfully and more deeply. I have a good friend who once said this about his marriage: "The secret to midlife marital happiness is not about staying the same. It's about falling in love again. That's what I'm experiencing. I didn't know Sheri when we first got married like I do now. It was attraction, and she seemed to like me enough. Now I'm falling in love with little things, weird things. We are talking more and making different efforts. But I didn't know what falling in love meant when it was hormonal. Now it's everything—mind, heart, body, soul. That's been *the* most exciting discovery for me."

In my college days, I often walked with my friends through the center of campus, and when a good-looking woman walked past us, one of the guys typically whispered, "I'm in love." I know, women, it sounds incredibly shallow, and it was. But it's still the truth. At one time or another, we all have had our brains hijacked by hormones that fuel passion and romance. The feelings are euphoric and amazing, but that elation in your brain fades and often the sparks that drew you together are not the sparks that create a long-lasting, beautiful relationship of connection, intimacy, and contentment.

The empty-nest years do not need to look the way they are sometimes represented—a bored, sad, and lonely couple sitting at the kitchen table, frustrated and mumbling, "Why don't the kids call?" Here is some good news: research reveals there is an uptick in marital satisfaction among empty-nest couples. When you compare couples the same age, fifty to seventy years old, the couples in the empty nest report greater happiness and marital satisfaction than couples with kids still in the home.[11] I know that to be true for Cathy and me. Our empty-nest season has been a time of rediscovery in our relationship, of finding intimacy again and keeping it alive, choosing lasting romance and relationship. A healthy second-half marriage can be better than the first half if you are willing to put in the time and energy it takes to make it thrive.

Some couples blossom in the empty nest, and others wilt. If you had a strong marriage before the kids moved out, you won't feel the loss as much as if you had a weak marriage. It makes sense that kid-centered or what some call child-focused marriages make it harder to stay connected once the children leave home. In a weak marriage, issues often become magnified in the empty nest. Perhaps a couple swept their issues under the carpet, avoiding the problems, while focusing on the kids. It's so easy to hide relational problems behind the children. In the empty nest, those ignored problems resurface around the time the kids leave home. A marriage in which the couple's relationship was not much of a priority will have lost its luster. This is when couples look across the table and feel like strangers. They aren't just dealing with anger and contempt or a lack of intimacy, but they find themselves fighting to keep the spark alive. These are the people who feel ignored, neglected, and sometimes a bit hopeless in their relationship. One woman said to me, "We are living alone together."

Though studies show an uptick in marital satisfaction among empty nesters, the divorce rate among US adults aged fifty and older has roughly doubled since the 1990s. Divorce has become less common for younger adults, while the so-called gray divorce is on the rise.[12] Where do you fit in? Is your marriage in the empty nest better or worse? Following are four principles to help your marriage thrive, even if you think it falls into the not-so-good category. It is quite normal to enter the empty nest with some major relational fatigue, but the good news is that you can bring the spark back. This season is the perfect time to shift the perspective of your relationship. So much of a relationship is habit, so habitual ways of thinking must be discarded for better ways. Remember, most games are won in the second half.

How to Thrive in the Second Half of Your Marriage

1. Now is the perfect time to reboot your marriage. No one has ever accused me of being a technology expert. True confession: our IT guy at HomeWord and my assistant mock me sometimes for my lack of understanding of technology. I use it every day, but I just don't totally understand how it works. But I've learned a secret to success with technology. The most effective first thing to do with a malfunctioning gadget is to unplug it, wait ten seconds, and then plug it back in. I've learned that 50 percent of my tech problems just need a reboot.

Guess what? The empty nest is the perfect time to reboot your marriage. Most couples I know in this stage say that at midlife, they had to acknowledge the drift in their marriage and the need for a course correction. Sometimes the correction is drastic, and other times it is minor. Maybe a midlife crisis or two has caused a lack of connection or even boredom. We must look at rebooting as a good thing. Just as there was a transition toward parenthood within the marriage, there is a transition away from day-to-day parenting during this phase. The reboot includes new roles and adjustments.

Authorities suggest that once the final kid leaves home, or even is in the preparation phase, every couple should sit down and ask important questions. What's next for our relationship? Do we have any dreams for us as a couple? What makes us saddest about the kids being gone? What are we most looking forward to in our new relationship? Are there any roles we can share that we didn't share before? What can we do to have more intimacy and connection in our relationship? What's good about our relationship? What needs improvement? What is missing? What is confusing? Part of rebooting in marriage is adjusting to new roles and embracing new opportunities to draw closer to each other.

William and Cynthia heard me speak at a marriage conference where I shared this phrase that a woman had shared with me: "Untended fires soon become nothing but a pile of ashes." After my talk, they approached me and asked, "What if the fire was untended for so long that the ashes are cold?"

I quoted something that I had read by a couple I respect greatly, David and Claudia Arp: "Logs don't move on their own; if a fire is to keep going, someone has to stoke it. This is true in our love life—especially in the second half of marriage."[13]

They asked, "What would you do?"

I said, "I would stoke the fire—whatever that means for you."

They saw me the next year at the same marriage conference. They walked up to me holding hands. "We took your advice and we have had a 'restart' on our marriage." They told me that their relationship had never been stronger.

When I asked how they stoked the fire, they said it wasn't just one thing but taking several smaller steps toward each other. It was time well invested in weekly dates, more physical intimacy, walks, and coffees. It was spending more time talking and dreaming together, some minor adjustments that made all the difference. The love was there. It just needed a reboot. Now they're calling the reboot their encore marriage.

2. Fireworks have nothing on friendship. There is a classic scene in an old-time movie titled *Shenandoah*. Charlie Anderson, played by the amazing Jimmy Stewart, has a conversation with his daughter's boyfriend, Sam. In the film, Sam asks Charlie for permission to marry his daughter. The conversation goes like this:

Sam: I want to ask for your daughter's hand in marriage.

Charlie: Why? Why do you want to marry her?

Sam: Well, I love her.

Charlie: That's not good enough. Do you *like* her?

Sam: I just said I—

Charlie: No, no. You said you loved her. There is some difference between love and like. You see, Sam, when you love a woman without likin' her, the night can be long and cold, and contempt comes up with the sun.[14]

No doubt passion and romance are part of a healthy marriage, but it's proven that companionship and deep friendship are often the best predictors of happiness in a long-lasting relationship. From painful experience, many people know you can love someone and have a horrible relationship. It's when you *like* them that your love relationship deepens. Liking your spouse involves turning toward your spouse with positivity. Positivity involves the emotional climate of your relationship. Dr. John Gottman, one of the world's leading marriage researchers, claims that one of the main differences between a stable and an unstable marriage is spouses' positivity toward one another. As it turns out, positivity is a choice. Couples in the happiest and most fulfilled marriages don't seem to have any fewer problems than others, but they do tend to choose to be more positive. Life is more about perspective than circumstance. Couples who choose positivity and work on friendship have happier relationships.

Having a friendship is key to a long-lasting relationship. Dr. Georgia Witkin puts it this way: "In survey after survey, at least 80 percent of couples in successful long-term relationships report that they had become best friends."[15] Best friends bring out the best in each other. They feel accepted. They enjoy each other's company. They have a companionate love on which their relationship is built. This creates emotional intimacy, which often precedes deeper attraction, passion, and physical intimacy.

3. Doing things together is sexy. Be purposeful about connection with your spouse. I love what Mary Jenson writes about her empty-nest marriage: "The kids are gone, the dogs are dead, and Ron and I are dating again."[16] Obviously, it's sad about the dogs, and I'm sure she had to work through the kids being gone, but what she is saying is, "We are going to celebrate this second half of our lives by being proactive in our relationship with regular dates." The couples who do well in the second half put renewed energy into doing things together. Rob and Judy share a love for cool, funky coffee shops. They made a list of twenty-seven coffee shops in, of all places, the state of Iowa. They try to visit one a week. I'm sure they enjoy the coffee, but it's really about the experience. The last time I checked, Rob said they had already been to fourteen coffee shops, and the farthest one was four hours away from their home. They call their visits "adventure coffee outings." I have a feeling those coffee times are more about the journey than the destination. Yes, it can be sexy just to do things together.

One of my favorite books on the empty nest was written by Melissa Shultz, *From Mom to Me Again*. Melissa writes on health and parenting for the *New York Times*, the *Washington Post*, *Reader's Digest*, and more. This book is about her surviving the first year of her empty nest and reinventing the rest of her life. I love how she writes about her reconnection with her husband.

> I know my husband well. I can tell you what shoes he'll pick out to buy, the TV shows he watches, the toothpaste he uses, and that breakfast will always be a bowl of Rice Chex mixed with Corn Flakes. But I also know there's more to him than that. I know this because there's more to me than my breakfast choices, the side on which I part my hair, and the color of my shirts (coral). After years of living in the family-focused world we created—the roles we've played thus far as parents, and the way we've interacted—well, that world is no longer.

So how do I know all this? It's not therapy. It's the Corner Bakery. We've been learning about one another again over Saturday lunch at our neighborhood Corner Bakery. I order the same thing, and he likes to shake it up. We always share a dessert, whatever is new on the menu. And we take our time. Sometimes two hours or more. In the history of being us, this never happened until we started to transition to the empty nest. At first, we didn't have much to talk about other than our kids. Now we talk about everything and nothing at all.[17]

She goes on to say, "We're still here together because we want to be. And though we are married to each other, neither of us is married to the way we've always done things."

Isn't that what we are all looking for? Deeper connection and good times together? My friends Jon and Theresa started walking their dog together every night. Before they began this habit, one would do the dishes and the other would walk the dog, for efficiency's sake. But when they decided to walk the dog together, what was once a chore became a time of deeper connection.

As you move into the empty nest, you are free to do things as you did before kids, like spontaneously go to the movies, play tennis, have a romantic encounter, or do nothing. If you don't have a regular date night, the kids can no longer be the excuse. You and everyone else in the world have

168 hours in the week. How about spending just 1 percent of that time on a planned date with your spouse? Couples who date regularly tend to have better relationships and more romance. What's holding you back?

When Cathy and I entered the empty nest for about the eighth time, we decided to put more adventure into our lives. You probably remember the old proverb "All work and no play makes Jack a dull boy." We have found that without some planned spontaneity in our relationship, we can work too much, which can lead to becoming bored with each other or just being boring. An adventure doesn't have to be a fancy trip. It just needs to be creative, refreshing, and something that brings you and your spouse energy.

As much as I enjoy having a book published, I dread the process of research and writing. I certainly identify with British novelist George Orwell when he said, "Writing a book is a horrible, exhausting struggle like a long bout of some painful illness. One would never undertake such a thing if he were not driven on by some demon you can neither resist nor understand."

In the middle of one of the worst days of writing this book, I got a text from Cathy.

Cathy: Jim, how about when you finish writing this book, we take a couple of days and go to spring training?

Jim: What? I had no idea you would ever want
to go to spring training. You have never
mentioned that once in your life!

Cathy: Well, it's not exactly on my bucket list. But
it could be fun. As long as we don't go to more
than one game a day.

Jim: Great. Let's do it.

My worst day of writing instantly became my best day of
writing. Why? I could look forward to an adventure. Cathy
was making the sacrifice, but she also knows that a baseball
game takes about three hours of a twenty-four-hour day. So
the adventure wasn't as much about baseball as it was about
connection. Yes, doing things together is sexy, even if it's
watching a baseball game. And to prove that this was a sacrifice on Cathy's part, I still have the photo on my phone
of a time when we were sitting together at a playoff game
between the Los Angeles Dodgers and their archrival, the
San Francisco Giants, and my daughter took a picture of
Cathy fast asleep on my shoulder.

**4. Every great love story is a never-ending conversa-
tion.** I'm in complete agreement with Winston Churchill
when he said this about his wife: "My most brilliant achieve-
ment was my ability to persuade my wife to marry me." But
even though Cathy and I write and speak on marriage and
have been married for more than forty-six years, we have a

high-maintenance marriage. We are both communicators, but when it comes to communicating with each other, we are sometimes like strangers passing in the night. We are very different from each other and tend to drive each other crazy. All our marriage, Cathy has wanted me to talk more with her from the heart. She craves emotional connection on a different level than I do.

Here is what we have found with communication in the empty nest. It's a time to either recover from some of the poor habits of communication with your spouse or repeat them. What would it look like for you to unlearn some poor habits? Here is a challenge to keep in front of you: every great love story is a never-ending conversation. For Cathy and me, we had to learn to create dedicated, nonnegotiable time to talk and listen.

Dedicated times to talk and listen don't just happen. You must make them happen. I know a couple who commute to work separately. They leave at the same time every day and call each other as they drive twenty minutes to work. One couple told me that when the kids were in the house, they took fifteen minutes after dinner just to sit on their love seat and reconnect. Now in the empty nest, they continue that practice. Some people walk their dog together, others do a coffee date. Not every conversation is breathtaking, but it is part of a continuous conversation that deepens a relationship. Too often the television, computer, social media, and other distractions break apart the needed emotional commitment. Do you really need to watch another news program? Isn't spending some time with your spouse much more rewarding?

Cathy and I had to learn that closeness comes in the magic of dialogue. A healthy dialogue with your spouse isn't merely dealing with the day-to-day responsibilities of marriage and family. A dialogue that is deeper, more open, drawing you together as a couple is sometimes sharing your dreams and hopes, along with your hurts. No one else in your life should share as much meaningful dialogue with you as your spouse. A spouse seldom falls into the temptation of an adulterous relationship because of sex appeal. It's usually because someone else is giving more of their heart in dialogue and sharing at a deeper level. The magic of more meaningful dialogue is in asking questions like, "What needs do you have right now where I could be more available?" and, "Where do you hope we are in our relationship three years from now?" Communication is much more about showing kindness, empathy, and respect than it is simply about words. Good communication is sharing your feelings and asking open-ended questions while discussing dreams and needs. Good communication is a learned trait, and it doesn't come naturally. You don't improve your communication by chance. It's by choice.

Someone once said, "You get what you repeat." You

deepen your marriage by repeating over and over again the steps that take you toward intimacy. If there are major roadblocks, take steps to unlearn and unblock. Sometimes that requires the help of a counselor, marriage book, or conference. I've found in my own life that when I lean toward intimacy and connection, it eventually becomes second nature. Henry Ford was asked about building a car. His answer makes a lot of sense: "Nothing is particularly difficult if you do it over and over again." I recently asked a couple who were part of the 4 percent of couples who make it to more than sixty years in marriage what was the key to their marital success. The woman didn't hesitate: "Show love, grace, kindness, forgiveness, and affection today, and then repeat that day after day for the next sixty years."

Communication Questions for Deeper Discussion

1. How would you respond to this phrase: "How your spouse treats you is their issue. How you respond is yours"?

2. It is important to give each other space in the empty nest. Do you agree or disagree?

3. Kindness matters. Kindness is a critical element of a successful second half of marriage. How are you doing in this area?

4. How can you reconnect with your spouse emotionally and physically?

5. Are you a safe person for your spouse?

6. Are there mentors, peers, pastors, or counselors who could help you draw closer to each other in this phase of your lives?

7. What are some of your unmet expectations?

8. In what ways do you take your spouse for granted?

9. What roles do you and your spouse need to redefine in this new phase of life?

10. How well are you handling conflict in your marriage?

11. Do you have any unresolved anger or resentment?

12. How well are you dealing with change?

Your Marriage Has a Soul

For more than three years, when I was in my twenties, I went to lunch every Wednesday with one of my spiritual mentors. His impact on my life will last for eternity. We would sit down and he would look me right in the eyes, as if he were looking inside of me, and ask me the same awkward question every week: "Jim, how is the condition of your soul?" That question always made me feel uncomfortable. I never really figured out how to answer adequately. If I said good, I didn't want him to think I wasn't aware of my brokenness. And if

I said bad, I was afraid he would think I was breaking each of the Ten Commandments on a regular basis. Each week, I mumbled something incredibly inarticulate, and we moved on. He was always loving, welcoming, and filled with grace.

Long after he moved and we quit meeting, I learned that our souls are intricately connected to our hearts, minds, bodies, and spirits. Our souls are integrated with all aspects of our being. Our souls have the capacity to bring our lives and relationships toward a healthy place. They are the center of our inner lives. A healthy soul brings together goodness and intimacy in a relationship. An unhealthy soul brings clutter, chaos, brokenness, and pain. I believe that your marriage has a soul as well. I'm not a theologian, so I can't totally explain it, but I think Jesus gave us a hint of this when he said, "For this reason a man will leave his father and mother and be united to his wife, and the two will become one flesh. So they are no longer two, but one flesh. Therefore what God has joined together, let no one separate" (Matt. 19:5–6).

Three words:

- **United.** To be united means to be bonded. Bondedness can imply a sexual bonding, but it's so much more than that. It's about a deep connection, being yoked, fusion, and intimacy. That can happen only when the soul of your marriage is good.
- **One flesh.** To be one flesh means to be "glued

together." Yes, this can also be a sexual term, but once again, it can be so much more. This is about sharing your lives together, possessions, children, joy, and pain. It's the joining of your souls spiritually.

The goal of the second half of marriage is to become more united, more one, than ever before. It's a chance for new beginnings and building on the foundation you already have established for your marriage. No one said it would be easy, but in the end, you will be able to say, "Falling in love with my spouse and staying in love is one of the best things that ever happened to me." I've heard it said that a successful and beautiful marriage is falling in love many times, always with the same person. Don't forget that the game is usually won in the second half.

Cathy and I were fortunate to learn about the soul of our marriage from a mentoring couple we had the privilege of regularly spending time with. I've always thought that the least developed area of intimacy for most couples is spiritual intimacy. Even though we have spent all of our adult lives together, this was true for us. I asked this beautiful couple what they did to enhance their spiritual intimacy. Their answer surprised me with its simplicity. They said, "We spend twenty minutes a week reading the Bible, praying together, and sharing with each other how God has been working in our lives." It sounded a bit spiritually wimpy to me, but then, Cathy and I didn't have a set time to do even twenty minutes. As we were pulling out of our mentors' driveway that night, Cathy said to me, "I'd like to do that twenty minute a week thing." We now call it our closer time. It's usually not a big deal. It's simple. We read a Scripture passage or an inspirational devotional. We pray together. Over the years, our closer time has helped us work on the soul of our marriage as well as anything has. What about you? What are you doing to enhance the soul of your marriage? The kids aren't the excuse anymore. Most of us have the time. It's a matter of leaning into it and making it happen regularly.

Who would have thought that the most intimate times in a marriage aren't necessarily in the first few years but in the empty nest? In the second half, when you work at staying in love, the spark can continue, glow even brighter, and bring a warmth of intimacy that can happen only when you are willing to devote the time, energy, and attention not to settle for a mediocre relationship. You can be more united and experience more of an authentic oneness than you ever imagined.

Chapter 5

REKINDLING ROMANCE

Principle 5: Untended embers soon become ashes. But a spark can reignite the fire.

"We are moving our sex life from the back burner to the front, and it looks different with changing libidos."

I recently saw a cartoon of an empty-nest couple in the living room of their home. She is sitting reading a book and he is standing next to her. He says to his wife, "Now that the kids are grown and gone, I thought it might be a good time for us to have sex." It made me smile because that seems to be the joke about the empty nest: it's less than romantic. But it doesn't have to be that way. My research about the empty-nest years and my conversations with empty-nest couples reveal something different. I keep hearing that in the second-half years, couples rekindle their romance and now enjoy deeper and more meaningful intimacy. Why is it that for some couples the second half loses its romantic spark and for others romance moves from the back burner to the front? Romance is much more than sex, but a healthy sexual relationship with your spouse is undoubtedly one of the key expressions of a close loving relationship. As my friend Kevin Leman says, "If you think sex isn't important, you are badly mistaken."

Do you know people who don't have much of a filter and often say things that make you smile, cringe, or just shake your head and wonder? I do. When I began to speak about romance in the empty nest, I seemed to attract more of these people than normal. "We haven't had sex in twelve years. Is that a problem?" "Ever since the kids left the house, she wants to make love all the time. I just can't keep up with her!" "My husband wants me to watch porn with him. He says it will enhance our relationship." "Sex is boring." "Can you remind me what sex is? It has been so long I can't remember." I'm usually not speechless, but all these statements give me pause. No matter what your experience is or where you are in the romance department, the empty nest is a perfect time to work on rekindling romance.

Notice that I carefully used the word *work*. When you

got married, that probably wasn't the first word that came to mind when you thought about romance, but if you think your romance could use a little rekindling, you are not alone. Most people attending our conferences or participating in our empty-nest focus groups report a greater desire for deeper romance and physical intimacy than they are experiencing. Maybe you're the same?

What would you like your romance to look and feel like in the second half? If it's going great, stay with it. If it could use rebooting, why not start today? Who would have ever thought that sex and romance would be complicated? But it is true that for many, it is quite complex. I've met hundreds of empty nesters who say that they were able to move sex and romance from the back burner to the front with a new focus on having a vibrant relationship. While I can't promise fireworks and choirs of angels every time, I believe that physical intimacy was created by God and that in the second half it can be more beautiful than in the first. Jesus said it best: "And the two will become one flesh." One flesh is not just a feeling but a sense of oneness that brings a mysterious and profound joy. Writer and philosopher Frederick Buechner writes, "Contrary to [what some believe], sex is not sin. Contrary to Hugh Hefner, it's not salvation either. Like nitroglycerin, it can be used either to blow up bridges or heal hearts."[18] Let's strive for a marriage with healed hearts of oneness. Now that's a worthy goal. It's not always easy, but the process toward oneness is possible. My friend Lu Williams says, "The sexual relationship between a husband and wife is the beating heart of a marriage. Sexual intimacy bonds the God-ordained union and sets it apart from every other earthly relationship. A happy, healthy sex life and marriage bond secures a family."[19]

Let's look at how to rekindle romance in the second half.

Rekindling Romance

1. Pleasure: Sex is fun! Do you enjoy your sexual relationship with your spouse? Unless there are medical or physical complications, you should be taking delight in your physical intimacy. Far too many empty nesters tell me that their physical intimacy has lost its luster. It's time to change that and move to meaningful enjoyment. You may have to get rid of some of the weird tapes in your head when it comes to enjoying sex with your spouse. One woman confided in me that she could still hear her mother's voice telling her as a teenager, "Don't do it. It's dirty, rotten, ugly, and sinful. Save it for the one you love." Somehow the dirty, rotten, ugly, and sinful stuck with her even in her marriage, and things weren't going so well in her mind. The mind is the most powerful sex organ. Sex is meant to be a uniting act, and it's meant to be pleasurable. God is the creator of males and females, and that means he created our sexuality and wants us to enjoy sexual intercourse. He created sex to be pleasurable.

God created most men to enjoy it so much that they think about it a lot. It's often their favorite activity. This may be a generalization, but a man can be asleep in bed with a headache or toothache or even be having a near-death experience, but if his wife gives him the sign, he is ready for pleasure. God created what some people call the "pleasure spot" (clitoris) in a woman. God was the one who put the pleasure spot there for what appears to be pure enjoyment. You were meant to enjoy physical intimacy with your spouse. This sets the marriage relationship apart from every other relationship. Unfortunately, emotional distance, anger, resentment, and exhaustion can be strong blocks to the beauty of physical intimacy. Since sexual intimacy is more than just pleasure, we often have to deal with emotional barriers before we can experience purposeful pleasure. (More on that later in the chapter.)

2. Connection: Emotional intimacy almost always precedes good physical intimacy. Good sex begins with your clothes on. We develop sexual intimacy by understanding that without emotional intimacy and connection, there will be little interest in developing sexual intimacy. This means taking time to connect, talk, and nurture your relationship. A woman enjoying her empty-nest years once told me, "My husband has no idea how two things he does gets me ready for sexual intimacy." I asked her what those two things were. She answered, "When he gives me time and touch." I asked her what made those two things so important. She said, "We've been sitting in our back yard after dinner many nights and just enjoying time talking with each other. And for touch, it's the nonsexual touch. When he takes my hand or puts his arm around me." She added with a smile, "Also when he touches the dishes or the vacuum. A clean house is foreplay." Marriage expert and author Gary Chapman once told me, "If I'd known a clean toilet was so important to my wife, I'd have cleaned the toilet daily."

Who would have thought that after the honeymoon, we would need to nurture romance with meaningful emotional connection? The emotional climate you help produce in the home creates or destroys opportunities for meaningful, intimate lovemaking. Even talking about your sexual relationship can be emotionally connecting. Many couples tell us at our conferences that they have not talked about their sexual relationship in several years. Intimate conversations produce deeper connection, which leads to a stronger desire for sexual intimacy as well.

3. Initiative: Just say yes! Don't wait. Initiate. I know this is a rather corny phrase, but it is true. Back to those tapes in our head. Women, one of the greatest gifts you can give your husband is to initiate sex. Men have a deep need to feel wanted and to please you. Do you realize that if a woman tells her husband in the morning that she hopes to have physical intimacy with him later that evening he will be thinking about it all day long? It's the anticipation that makes it even more special. As discussed in the previous section, men can often initiate with their wives simply by meeting their emotional needs. As people get older, sometimes they miss out on the fun of flirting and pursuing. One woman told me, "I like being intimate with my husband, but sometimes he is just way too direct and makes me feel like it is more of a transaction than a loving gesture of intimacy." Sometimes these three words—talk, listen, and empathy—are difficult for men, but even an attempt can make a huge difference.

You are never too old to flirt. The verb *to flirt* means "to behave as though attracted to or trying to attract someone." Who doesn't want to feel like they are attractive to their spouse? My friend Doug Fields tells women that "taking off any item of clothing is flirting. A smile, a nod, a wink, basically walking in front of your husband is flirting." Flirting can be a passionate kiss or whispering something to your spouse that no one else can hear when you're out with her or him.

I have a friend who is a type-A personality. From what he tells me, he works too many hours. His wife says he is driven and distracted. He hardly noticed that his wife was having trouble in their empty-nest phase because he was busy making his next highly successful business deal. In his mind, he was doing it all for his wife and family. In her mind, their marriage was in a flat spot, a rut. One day after a particularly difficult and negatively charged evening of tension with his wife, he realized he had some changing to do if they were going to rekindle their romance and their marriage. He called his wife while she was at work and invited her to have dinner at their home. And he was going to prepare the meal.

Because he never cooked, his wife was a bit skeptical, but she was curious. He canceled all of his work activities for the afternoon. He went to the mall and bought some Godiva chocolates, a sweater, and for the first time in his life, some lingerie for his wife. Since he was a lousy cook, he ordered takeout from her favorite Italian restaurant. He set the table with their best dishes and some candles and turned on some soft romantic music. Most significant, he put aside the other pressing issues of his life so he could totally focus on her.

She came home tired and somewhat distracted. After she got over the shock of seeing the transformed dining room and all that her husband had done, her mood changed. When my friend told me the story, I asked how the evening went. He smiled and said, "None of your business!" I think that meant it was a great romantic evening because he showed some initiative and met his wife's needs. This became a defining moment in their marriage, rewiring their understanding of each other.

4. Libido: Most couples have different sex drives. Your libido is your sex drive, and by the time you are an empty nester, there is a good chance that the libido of at least you or

your spouse has slowed a bit because of menopause, low tes-
tosterone, chronic tiredness, or any number of other issues.
It is important to stay in touch and be aware of each other's
sex drives. No matter where you are on the scale, it is an act
of love to show tenderness and patience and even to compromise when it comes to physical intimacy. Although it's easy
to generalize, in most cases the male sex drive is stronger
than the female. That's not just a cultural phenomenon, it's
a proven medical fact. It's important to understand some of
the differences between men's and women's sex drives.

Studies report that sexual desire in women is extremely
sensitive to "environment and context." A woman's sexual
desire usually is the barometer of her world. If she is not
rested, happy, healthy, and feeling appreciated, supported,
and loved, she is not going to feel like having sex. Women
often comment that their sexual desire begins between their
ears, not in their private parts. Men on the other hand don't
seem to be as sensitive to their environment. Men like to
have sex to feel emotionally connected, and women need
to feel emotionally connected to have sex. As you begin to
understand your spouse's needs and desires and how your
spouse gets to a place of seeking physical intimacy, your sexual relationship becomes much more fulfilling. Too many
empty nesters have told me that they just didn't put much
energy into their physical intimacy during the kid years.
Sometimes you need to tell your spouse what you need and

want. Although more women than men are better at being in touch with their emotional health, women will occasionally come up to me at a conference and say something like, "My husband isn't spontaneous or romantic anymore." I often respond by saying, "Have you told him what you need and what you want?" They look at me as if something is wrong with my question and say, "Of course not. Aren't they just supposed to know that?" The answer is that most men do want to please their wives, but unfortunately many just don't know what their wives need or want. My suggestion is always the same: "Tell them." This may be the first step in helping them to understand your libido. The same goes for men.

What empty nesters are learning is that you don't always have to be in the mood before agreeing to have sex. It isn't supposed to be like sampling medicine. Even if you aren't in the mood, you can be surprised by the pleasure and connection it brings. I was speaking at a conference in Hawaii about teaching your children healthy sexuality. Before the talk, I had breakfast with a wonderful couple who was also speaking at the event. The woman told me she was coming to my workshop. She said they had five kids, and neither she nor her husband had their parents talk to them about sex when they were kids. Then she just blurted out, "Jack and I schedule our sexual intimacy every Wednesday." Jack had his spoon of oatmeal halfway up to his mouth when he stopped and just looked at his wife as if to say, "I can't believe you just told him about our sex schedule." I think I surprised them by affirming them. It's something they can both look forward to and cherish. Though I'm sure they have missed a few Wednesdays, the schedule became a beautiful tradition of their relationship. They may have had mismatched sex drives, but not on Wednesdays.

5. Respect: Be a lover, not a parent. No one wants to be physically intimate with their parents. It's always a good idea to back off the parenting-your-spouse program and treat him or her like your lover. Your spouse needs you to be their cheerleader and not a coach. They once were your girlfriend or boyfriend, then you were engaged, and finally they became your spouse, but they are not your child. I remember an intense conversation in my office with a couple in which the wife screamed, "I'm not your mother!" The husband came right back, "Then quit trying to mother me." Nagging doesn't work. Shaming doesn't work. Sometimes even unsolicited advice doesn't work. Don't be the person who says to another adult (your spouse), "Put your coat on. It's cold outside." That is what you say to a seven-year-old, not your spouse. Your role as lover is far more important than trying to fix your spouse. You can fix yourself, but quit trying to fix your spouse, because negativity and nagging are not parts of your role. Experience is always a better teacher than advice, so if it's cold and they don't put their coat on, let them experience the cold outside, and not in your relationship.

6. Hindrances: "Not tonight. I have a hangnail."
Through the years, we often build up hindrances to a healthy romantic relationship. Occasionally we need to unlearn our poor or lazy habits. Little things can become big things if they are left unaddressed. What was once a minor aggravation is now keeping a couple from intimacy. If it has been many years of lack of focus or if there are unaddressed issues or unmet desires, perhaps the best thing you can do is to seek professional advice and counsel. If there are addictions or infidelity in the past, then you most certainly need a good counselor. Don't be afraid to ask for help.

One of the primary hindrances couples talk about are the kids. Since the kids aren't in the home anymore, maybe it's time to take a closer look at what is holding you back. The couples who do well with romance are still learning after all these years. They are proactively having adventures toward deeper intimacy. They are creative and keep their sexual relationship fresh, which is one of the best aphrodisiacs for healthy physical intimacy.

Surveying those who have attended HomeWord's Refreshing Your Marriage conferences, we have learned that the following are the top eight killers of passion and sex:

1. **Exhaustion and stress.** Perhaps the greatest hindrance to sexual intimacy is the breathless pace of our lives. Sure, there will always be times when we

are tired, but being too tired constantly means we have our priorities in the wrong place.

2. **Lack of physical affection, flirting, and intimate conversation.** Couples who say their romance isn't working are typically relationally lazy or unwilling to put any effort into their romance. Do not ever allow sex to become routine.

3. **Too much to do and too many things left undone.** A good principle to remember is that when you are overcommitted, you are probably underconnected.

4. **Emotional distance and intense conflict.** Unresolved anger, conflict, and negativity cause emotional distance. This is a major passion killer. It takes discipline and good communication skills to leave your anger out of the bedroom. As I said, good counseling is never a bad idea.

5. **Lack of physical or emotional safety.** If a person does not feel safe with their spouse on any level, there will be little interest in physical or emotional intimacy.

6. **Feeling unappreciated.** Mark Twain said, "I can live two months on one good compliment." Appreciation, affirmation, and affection produce intimacy. Feeling as though you are being taken for granted produces only a lack of desire. Rodney Dangerfield once joked, "It's tough to stay married. My wife kisses the dog on

the lips, yet she won't drink from my glass." I hope you never can relate to that.

7. **Negativity and constant criticism.** Constant criticism, even if it's true, will not produce closeness in a relationship. Nagging and negativity are the worst motivators.

8. **The "plumbing" isn't working correctly.** If a man or woman is experiencing physical issues related to physical intimacy, it's time to get checked out by a doctor. There is help and hope in most cases for whatever is going on. A couple in one of our empty-nest focus groups smiled when they said, "As we grew older, K-Y Jelly made all the difference in the world."

Over the years as I have shared these sex and passion killers, it has become clearer to me that many of those issues go hand in hand. One thing for sure is that if we are going to rekindle romance in the second half of our lives, we most likely will need to tweak or reinvent some of the ways we approach our relationship with our spouse. If you identified with a few or even one of these passion killers, then perhaps it's time to be courageous enough to ask for help. A marriage tune-up with a counselor, marriage mentors, or even good friends is never a bad idea. I challenge couples to read one marriage book or to go to one marriage conference a year. You can always learn something to improve your relationship.

How to Improve Your Sex Life

In a study of nearly 100,000 couples from all over the world, researchers found that couples' satisfaction with their sex lives tended to have something to do with specific acts of love.[20] What is so interesting to me about these results is that these acts of love are all actions anyone can take to improve their relationship. The study's findings are closely related to what has already been covered in this chapter.

Couples who are deeply satisfied with their sex lives:

- Say "I love you" to their spouse every day and mean it.
- Buy one another surprise romantic gifts.
- Compliment their spouse often.
- Invest time and money in romantic vacations.
- Give one another back rubs.
- Kiss one another passionately and for no reason at all.
- Show affection in public (handholding, kissing, caressing).
- Cuddle with one another almost every day. (Only 6 percent of the noncuddlers claimed they had great sex lives.)
- Have romantic dates once a week that may include lovemaking.
- Make having sex a priority and learn to talk comfortably with each other about it.

What's remarkable about all these acts is that they are simple and provide connection with your spouse. Rekindling romance isn't as hard as we make it sound. It is accomplished with baby steps and experiencing something fresh in our relationship almost immediately. Yes, there are hindrances and we bring brokenness to a relationship, but healing and intimacy are ours if we invest the time and energy.

I love the story I heard about a woman from Houston, Texas, whose husband had recently passed away. She lovingly remembered that every Valentine's Day for the forty-six years of their marriage, her husband had bought her a beautiful bouquet of flowers. A few months after his death, on Valentine's Day she was shocked to receive the most gorgeous floral bouquet addressed to her from her husband. She was sure the florist had made a mistake, and it made her angry and heartbroken. Frustrated, she called the florist. The florist said, "No, ma'am, this was not a mistake. Before your husband passed away, he prepaid for many years and asked us to guarantee that you would continue to receive a bouquet every year on Valentine's Day." The attached card read, "My love for you is eternal."

I'll bet that husband *chose* to have a good marriage.

Chapter 6

MIDLIFE MELTDOWN OR

PURPOSEFUL LIVING?

❧

Principle 6: Find your purpose in midlife
and you will set the world on fire.

❧

*"There's finally time for me to pay more attention
to my own life, my purpose, and my passions."*

As you may be picking up on at this point, the empty-nest
phase of life is full of new opportunities, if you're willing
to see them. Most people simply don't realize how pivotal
moving into the empty nest can be. We were so busy and
distracted with kids, trying to make it through each week or
even the day, that very few of us prepared for our halftimes.

That's probably one of the major reasons for a midlife crisis or meltdown. There was just too little investment in this new season of life.

Sometimes a midlife crisis is characterized by the man buying a convertible sports car, wearing a gold chain around his neck, new designer clothes that don't seem to fit right, and a brand-new hairstyle, with a twenty-five-year-old girlfriend on his arm. Or the woman covering up her mourning of middle age with clothes, hair, and a lifestyle that might work for a twenty-year-old, but don't exactly fit her middle-aged body or way of life. Many people do feel lost in a passionless marriage or experience a loss of purpose after the kids leave home. Others may be in denial that they are having any kind of a midlife crisis.

A person having a midlife crisis might sound fine, but inside, they're going through something like this:

"Are you having a midlife crisis?"

"No." (Or at least if I am, I'm not ready to admit it.)

"But you are acting really weird."

"I'm just confused." (That's an understatement. Is this all there is to life? Am I stuck living like this for the rest of my days?)

"Confused about what?"

"I don't know. Just stuff." (My life, my future, you,

getting older, feeling lost.)

"Are you happy?"

"I don't know." (I'm not even sure who I am or
  where I'm going.)

The good news is that whether or not you're in meltdown mode, this is the perfect time to recalibrate your life and come out much better on the other side. Your empty-nest years can be about finding a beautiful new purpose, making course corrections, establishing a new identity, having fresh adventures, and rebooting your life for a more meaningful existence than you ever imagined. But it doesn't just happen. It takes intentionality and focus. It takes some midcourse corrections. Bob Buford, author of a great book called *Halftime*, once said, "The first half is noisy, busy, almost frenetic. It's not that you do not want to listen to that still, small voice. It's that you never seem to have enough time to do it."[21] The crisis comes when we continuously add to the busyness and never heed the silence or take the time to figure out how life can improve in the second half.

Halftime: Now What?

Putting some healthy energy, reflection, and focus into your new phase of life affords new opportunities. If you transition correctly, you have more time to focus on how you want to live your remaining years. Whether you are ready for it or not, you are pivoting from your life with kids in the house to a new life with your kids out of the house. It's a time of losing some of the past and gaining new perspective, of assessing your gifts and abilities to see where they now fit, of tossing out the old and bringing in the new. Change is often difficult, but it can also be exciting.

As I mentioned, my wife, Cathy, and I have not had the clear-cut empty-nest experience. We experienced the boomeranging of our kids more than a few times. As I look back, I think Cathy has done a really good job of reinventing herself. As our youngest was transitioning to adulthood, Cathy decided to do what she loved and was trained to do—teaching kids with learning challenges. She returned to teaching for eleven years. Then as grandchild number one was born, she realized her dream was to become a fully engaged grandma. She retired from teaching, and when our daughter went back to teaching, Cathy helped watch our grandson, James. When Charlotte arrived two years later, the house was even busier, but Cathy wouldn't change it. She has loved this new season in her life. At the same time, she decided to take on the leadership of an evening women's Bible study. She is following her passion.

Are you following your passion in your second half? Mark had made a lot of money in his first half but felt there was more to life than making money. At his halftime, he moved from chasing success to finding significance. He retired at the height of his career to gain more time with his wife, kids, and grandkids. He also began to invest three days a week to assist a major financial stewardship ministry in going international. I recently asked him how he was doing. His short answer: "No regrets." His longer answer was that he is in the most fulfilling and challenging time of his life. Anne, a single mom, went back to school to get her marriage-and-family counseling degree. Today she is fulfilling a dream that began in her mind right after college but was put on hold for twenty-two years.

Most halftime decisions aren't as dramatic, but your second half can be just as meaningful as you make the transition from a full nest to an empty one. And remember, you can't look at your second half through the lens of your first. It's a new day with new opportunities. It's time to make adjustments. Sometimes you take baby steps, and other times you take a leap of faith. To make the transition, you'll want to answer these questions:

- What is my passion?
- What in my life has gone unattended or uncultivated?
- What's next?
- What will my second half look like:
  - In my marriage (if married)?

- In my relationships with my adult children?
- In my vocation?
- In my faith and faith community?
- In my friendships and replenishing relationships?
- What do I need to give up to make progress?

Find Your Purpose

Have you seen the movie *City Slickers*, starring Billy Crystal as Mitch and Jack Palance as Curly? There is a section of significant dialogue in this hilarious comedy. Mitch has joined two other friends who come from the city to spend a couple of weeks driving a herd of cattle across the range on horseback. They all are experiencing midlife meltdowns in one form or another. These "city slickers" clearly have no idea what they are doing, and Curly, a shrewd cowboy, is their guide. As they are riding along the range, he gives Mitch some sage advice:

Curly: Yeah. You all come out here about the same age. Same problems. Spend fifty weeks a year getting knots in your rope, then you think two weeks up here will untie them for you. None of you get it. *Long pause.* Do you know what the secret of life is?

Mitch: No, what?

Curly: This. *Holds up an index finger.*

Mitch: Your finger?

Curly: *Shakes his head.* One thing. Just one thing. You stick to that and everything else don't mean s---.

Mitch: That's great, but what's the one thing?

Curly: That's what you've got to figure out.

Bob Buford found his one thing during his halftime. Bob was a successful businessman in the television industry. He considered making a change from pursuing success to gaining significance, but he was torn between living out his Christian faith and continuing with his work. Of course, he could do both, but he knew that if he was going to shift some time and attention from his career to move more to Christian ministry, he would have to make some major decisions and change his focus. Bob tells the story of paying a strategic-planning consultant thousands of dollars to help him find the answer.

The consultant was brilliant, demanding, and a devout atheist. Although the man didn't believe in God, Bob believes that God worked mightily through him. Bob and the consultant talked for hours. Bob was trying to figure out what he should do with the rest of his life and what could be most valuable. He told the consultant he was open to fresh endeavors, particularly in Christian leadership, but he was torn because he was making a lot of money and enjoying his work. The consultant finally spoke up. "I've been listening to you for a couple of hours," he said, "and I'm going to ask you what's in the box. For you, it's either money or Jesus Christ."

Bob said, "No one had ever put a significant question to me so directly." After much thought and undoubtedly some prayer, Bob told the consultant that if it had to be one or the other, he would put Jesus Christ in the box. From that time on, Bob shifted his purpose and aligned it with his faith passion. No, he didn't become another Mother Teresa, but his life's work, his relationship with his family, and his time, treasure, and talent became aligned with his one thing or his box.[22]

What's in your box? What's your one thing? Pursuing your one thing might require a dramatic switch or just a tweak. It's not so much about a job change as a heart change. My wife knew that for her, it was to be a fully engaged grandma. For my friend Rod, it was to stay involved in his business ventures and continue to be generous in his philanthropic endeavors. Deb moved from California to Texas to be closer to her children. Janet, a single mom, went back to school and became a marriage-and-family counselor. Your one thing isn't just about what you do. It's more about who you are. Someone once said to me, "The choices we make privately almost always have consequences that branch out publicly." The empty nest is not the time to plateau. It's the time to focus. If you have relatively good health, you might have decades of life remaining. Typically, it's not until the halftime of our lives that we have the energy to focus on that one thing.

A woman recently told me it was helpful for her to think about the words she wanted on her gravestone. I asked if she had it figured out yet. She said, "God first, family focused." She was making key decisions based on her passion and purpose. I wonder whether she had read Psalm 16:11: "You make known to me the path of life; you will fill me with joy in your presence, with eternal pleasures at your right hand." That sentence has quite a promise in it.

You might not feel like you have the time or energy to recalibrate your life. Most likely you're not sitting around with lots of time on your hands. If your cup is already overflowing, you may need to tip something out of it before you fill it with something new and more meaningful. Just this week, Cathy bought me a new shirt. I'm sure it will become one of my favorites. I found myself standing in front of my closet, looking at my old shirts, my "friends from the past." My philosophy is that when I get a new item of clothing, I dump an old one. For some reason, I was having trouble deciding what shirt to give away. I noticed a shirt that I hadn't worn in several years, but it did have some sentimental value. Then I realized I hadn't even thought about it for many years. Perhaps someone else would enjoy it, but I knew I wouldn't miss it.

It's the same with our lives. Your kids are out of the house. This means you have hours of time that you probably have dedicated to other things. If you have never done this, go through an exercise to determine what consumes your time and attention. I wouldn't be surprised if you found things that you'd be willing to dump. The principle is clear: you must let go of the old before you pick up something new.

Where do you start? How about with wasted time? Only you can decide where you are wasting time. Here are a couple of ideas. Open the settings on your phone and look at your screentime. Maybe you are spending too much time on social media. Do you watch the news? That's fine, but if you watch more than a half hour or an hour, isn't it much of the same thing repeatedly? I saved a lot of time when I quit watching the evening news. I get my fill of the news on the ten-minute drive to work and back. Not only has it saved time for other things, but it has also improved my stress level and mental health because I'm not getting sucked into the craziness of the twenty-four-hour news cycle. Is there a commitment you complain about but have kept doing because it's a habit? It's time to dump it.

Do you still need to work full time? Perhaps you do. I love my full-time work. But I realized I was packing too many hours into the week, so I cut back, and strangely enough, the stress load also lessened. There is a word in the English language that is the same in Spanish, and it's time for many of us halftimers to relearn it. It was one of our favorite words many years ago when our kids were in their terrible twos and threes. It's the word *no*. I guarantee you that with some introspection, you'll realize that there is something you have said yes to that really would have been better if you'd said no to. My wife used to have a favorite saying: "Jim, we have a messiah. He is doing very well. Don't replace him!" You might have to say no to some good things to say yes to the most important things in your life. Do it now while you have the energy and the focus.

Have a Different Kind of Adventure

And while you are at it, I hope you will make the second half more of an adventure than the first. In the first half, it's hard to have many adventures because of the daily busyness with kids, jobs, extended family, and everything else that is thrown our way. The second half provides more opportunities through the benefits of the empty nest. The problem is that sometimes the pace of life is addicting, and it is tough to stop and enjoy a new way of living. To make the second half better, we usually need to slow down, possibly even downsize and simplify. Only you know what that would look like for you. Sitting on the couch day after day watching old cooking shows or spending hours viewing the golf channel isn't my idea of adventure. Make the most of the extra time you have been given.

If you don't have time to create a bucket list for your second half, then I'm not sure your priorities are in the right place. As you create that bucket list, add activities or trips and fresh learning experiences. One of the things on my bucket list became the title of another book I wrote called *Have Serious Fun*. I wrote the words "have serious fun" and brainstormed with Cathy some adventures that would be fun for both of us. Maybe you have the money to buy a second home or go on a trip to the Holy Land. Perhaps fun is creating a bimonthly dinner tradition with your adult kids or designing a beautiful new garden. One woman wrote to us after one of our seminars saying she had been too busy to invest in meaningful peer relationships, so she was adding that to her list. For my good friends Tic and Terri, it was time to save money to go on their dream trip to Italy with their good friends Whittie and Robin. The two couples enjoyed planning it for a few years. Their motto for the trip, which our family has borrowed, was "No bad decisions. No wrong turns. No bad food."

What would your bucket list look like? What is holding you back?

The best years *can* be the second-half years if we do it right. It doesn't happen by circumstance and chance. We must become proactive to recalibrate our lives for the better. Recalibrate means "to change the way you do or think about something." There is a sign at my gym, which I need to frequent more often, that reads simply "No Regrets." I want to live that kind of a life. Speaker and sociologist Tony Campolo once spoke at a national pastors' conference in San Diego on a project that he and his students had just completed. They asked fifty people aged ninety-five and older a single question: "Do you have any regrets?" Here is what these beautiful people had to say:

1. **If I could do life over, I'd reflect more.** It's in the second half that we learn how important it is to find our strength in quietness and solitude. It's in times of reflection that our best answers come from somewhere deep within us. I have been a Christian for more than fifty years, and one of the first psalms I ever learned is this one: "Take delight in the LORD, and he will give you the desires of your heart" (Ps. 37:4). I find that when I am spending time in quiet reflection and delight with God, my priorities and passions come to the forefront. There is no shortcut to deeper reflection.

2. **If I could do life over, I'd risk more.** Moving out of your comfort zone in your family, in your vocation, and in so many other relationships in the second half is a risk. But these older people wouldn't hesitate to risk more often. It's with risk that we sometimes have our most important experiences. People who take risks in the second half don't seem to be afraid of

failure, because even if they do fail, they see the value in learning all the way through the risk. Someone once said, "It's risky not to take chances." We all know people who took risks and ended up changing the world. What risks would you take right now if you had the courage?

3. **If I could do life over, I would do more things that would live on after I'm dead.** I love this saying from the book of Ecclesiastes: "[God] has also set eternity in the human heart" (3:11). Time after time when I speak to older people, I hear things like, "I hope to make an eternal difference." What will your legacy be?

When I was younger, I spent most of my time speaking to middle school and high school students. I love what I do now, primarily working with parents and married couples, but it all started with those wonderful years of hanging out with kids. During one season of my life, I had the privilege to speak on most of the public high school campuses in the beautiful state of Hawaii. This opportunity came through the generosity of a couple who had already passed away but had left millions in their foundation to help families in their state succeed. The foundation hired me to come to Hawaii regularly to speak to kids and do a few marriage conferences. It was always so rewarding to see the fruit of this couple's labor continue even after they had died.

One time a woman came up to me after one of the school assemblies with tears in her eyes and said, "You are helping my mom and dad fulfill their lifelong dream to make an eternal difference." I didn't understand until she told me that she was this couple's daughter, the ones who'd set up the foundation. She said, "They worked so hard all their lives and made a lot of money, but they always told us kids, 'We will invest our money in eternity by helping young people make smart decisions.'"

Some of us who are never going to give away millions of dollars can still focus our time and attention on the spiritual legacy of our grandchildren or to teach a Bible study at our churches or to volunteer at a hospital or to do whatever is on our hearts to invest in something that will last long after we are gone. It is built within us to do that, and most often it happens during our second half.

In the second half, part of our destiny is to make sure that we do what Søren Kierkegaard, the Danish philosopher, theologian, and cultural critic, once wrote: "The thing is to understand myself, to see what God really wishes me to do . . . to find the idea for which I can live and die." As we make course corrections for more purposeful living in midlife, we move toward our encore, our legacy, making the most of the years we have left. This isn't time to stop running the race. It's time to live to the fullest and finish well.

Chapter 7

FINISHING WELL

❦

Principle 7: Do whatever it takes to make your top priorities your top priority.

*"Significance and a well-lived
life are not accidental."*

My friend Paul, who is in his late sixties, told me he once had a leader say to him, "I hope you are doing well as we sprint toward the finish line of life." Sprint? Really? Isn't life more like a marathon than a sprint? No one has ever suggested that I would make a good sprinter, ever. I wasn't fast in high school, and now that I'm in the empty nest, I'm even slower. But one of the biggest issues of life doesn't usually cross our minds until we hit the empty nest, and that is to finish the race well.

I'm not an expert at running marathons. I've run only one in my life. I finished it, but let's just say that my time was not going to take me to the Olympics—or even the Senior Olympics. When people asked about the marathon, they didn't ask about my time; they asked me, "Did you finish?" My pat answer was, "Yes, and standing up." Most runners sometimes experience tough times in a race, blisters, aches and pains, maybe a sprain or some other setback, but still their goal is to finish the race well. So it is in life. Since the game of life is usually won or lost in the second half, there may not be a more important goal than to finish well. The apostle Paul sums it up best: "I have fought the good fight, I have finished the race, I have kept the faith" (2 Tim. 4:7). What does finishing well mean to you in your marriage, if you are married? Or in your relationships with your adult children or with your grandkids? In your faith? In your work?

Saint Augustine suggested that the most important question regarding our legacy is, "What do I wish to be remembered for?"[23] He implied that when you can answer that question, you have achieved the beginning of adulthood. When we are on our deathbeds, we won't be asking about our retirement funds or the work we left undone. We will be asking questions like, "Was I faithful with the gifts God gave me? Was I faithful to my values, my faith, my family?" Finishing well is not about results but about faithfulness.

Living a life of faithful significance is not accidental. To live well is to live with purpose, mindful of a goal. For me, that goal centers much more on who I am than on what I do. But that was not always the case. So much of my self-esteem was wrapped up in my vocation, success, and recognition until I finally concluded that I wanted to make my goal to be able to say with Paul, "I have fought the good fight, I have finished the race, I have kept the faith." This doesn't mean we lose our drive or work ethic. It simply means that we have a higher purpose than our vocation or kids' success. This past year a few "superstars" of Christian leadership have stumbled in such huge ways as they neared the finish line. They had success in their careers, but they will be remembered for their lack of virtue and their failures rather than their life's work in ministry. That is not what you want for yourself.

How will you spend the productive years remaining to you to finish well in the important areas of your life? The path to finishing well is not found. It's most often made. You must create the most effective path to get you to the finish line with excellence. One of the greatest byproducts of finishing well is that your family and those closest to you can benefit from your good decisions. What do you dream of accomplishing in those twenty-five to thirty-five years you have left? Even if you don't have that many productive years left, what do you hope can happen with your life? This is where I lean into Scripture.[24] I love to read the books of Proverbs and Psalms for guidance on living productively.

These two books are part of what is called the Wisdom Literature of the Bible. Some people have been greatly inspired by reading one chapter of Proverbs and five psalms each day for a month for wisdom and direction. Since there are thirty-one chapters in Proverbs and 150 psalms, you can finish both books in a month.

The Scripture that has helped me most as I think about finishing well is in the New Testament, written by the author of Hebrews: "Therefore, since we are surrounded by such a great cloud of witnesses, let us throw off everything that hinders and the sin that so easily entangles. And let us run with perseverance the race marked out for us, fixing our eyes on Jesus, the pioneer and perfecter of faith. For the joy set before him he endured the cross, scorning its shame, and sat down at the right hand of the throne of God. Consider him who endured such opposition from sinners, so that you will not grow weary and lose heart" (Heb. 12:1–3).

This is what those few sentences have profoundly taught me about finishing well:

1. **Learn from other runners.** The writer of Hebrews mentions a "great cloud of witnesses." It's so important to learn from others. Are there people who positively influence you on a regular basis? If not, you are missing out on great opportunities to gain wisdom. The group of four men that I have met with every Tuesday

morning for the last eighteen years has given me such great wisdom and knowledge. These men help me with my judgment. I'm a better husband, father, and leader because of those Tuesday mornings. Find your group of men or women who are your replenishing relationships. Do you have mentors? Mentors are effective in business, but I find that mentors for marriage, parenting, and spiritual focus can make you a better person. Some of my mentors are younger than me, and others I "met" after they died, by reading the wisdom in their books.

2. **Run light.** The writer of Hebrews also talks about throwing off everything that hinders us and the sin that so easily entangles us. As I mentioned, Peter Drucker says, "First things first, last things not at all." As you run toward the finish line, is there anything you can do to run lighter and to remove obstacles that would keep you from finishing well? Stuff happens. Sometimes it's issues with our families, health, or circumstances over which we have no control. That's why we need to run light, saving the energy to have the right attitude about draining things that come our way, that sway us from our callings. I have a psychologist friend who always says, "Live your life at 80 percent." Doing so creates some margin in your life when tough times come your way.

3. **Run with perseverance.** Perseverance and grit help us overcome so many of our obstacles. Perseverance, endurance, grit, and courage are characteristics of people who have successful marriages, businesses, and relationships. I don't know anyone finishing well who doesn't possess these traits. Psychologist Angela Duckworth, in both her book and her Ted Talk about grit,[25] says her studies on high achievers in business and education reveal that success has almost nothing to do with talent but much more to do with a never-give-up attitude. She calls that attitude grit. Nobody said life would be easy, but the healthiest way to walk the path marked out for us is to combine our perseverance and passion with pure grit.

4. **Keep your eyes on the prize.** The prize for me goes back to the word *faithful*. That's what I want more than anything else—to remain faithful to God, my wife, my family, and my calling. The key to my being faithful is focusing on the foundation of my faith, which is trusting in Jesus. This is a simple but not easy decision. When I keep my eyes fixed on Jesus, things fall into place. I can handle the difficult circumstances life brings my way. But when I take my eyes off the prize, my focus becomes dim, and I can easily lose my way. I once asked a mentor who was nearing the end of his exemplary life, "What are you

doing to finish well?" He answered, "It doesn't start with my outside life; finishing well is an inside job." He quoted a great thinker, Dallas Willard: "If your soul is healthy, no external circumstance can destroy your life. If your soul is unhealthy, no external circumstance can redeem your life."

Stay Engaged with Your Soul

I must admit that during the first half of my life, I didn't think much about my soul. I knew I had one, but I was too busy and distracted to pay much attention to it. With my high-maintenance marriage to the love of my life, our kids' constant activities and needs, and a growing, busy, and sometimes struggling ministry, who could spend much time and energy thinking about soul care? For most, it's not until the second half of life, during the empty nest, that we realize that we have neglected the core of our being and the rest of our lives hangs in the balance. We realize we have neglected the eternal part of our lives because the temporal concerns of the world overpowered our soul care. And unfortunately, for many, the neglect is not without consequence. It is so true that a soul without a center finds its identity in meaningless externals. The result of an unhealthy soul is clutter, chaos, brokenness, and pain.

To finish well means to declutter your external life and

disengage from as many distractions as possible. I'm not suggesting you move to a distant island to live in a monastery, but I am suggesting that you invest in solitude, reading, reflection, and engaging your deeper life, which will help you to recover from your first half, allowing time to heal and create a more beautiful and meaningful second half. What are you doing to invigorate your soul? If the answer is "more of the same," then we can talk about the definition of insanity, which is doing the same thing over and over again expecting a different result. If anyone gives you a magic formula to invigorate your soul, don't trust them. Invigorating your soul is a process.

I'm still a work in process and will be for the rest of my life. But there is something I know. My friend John Ortberg calls it "soul keeping."[26] Soul keeping usually involves reading God's Word, worship, prayer, rest, gratitude, adoration, solitude, and meaningful conversation. Paul urged his protégé Timothy to "discipline yourself for the purpose of godliness" (1 Tim. 4:7 NASB). Part of leaning into your soul and finishing well is creating space in your life for the spiritual disciplines that build your foundation for dealing with whatever comes your way. For me, not only do I need to make a habit of certain practices that nourish my soul, but I need "thin places" to enhance that experience. Let me explain.

Find Your "Thin Places"

A thin place is a holy space where you encounter God's presence. It's a place where the boundary between heaven and earth is especially thin. No one really knows where the term originated, but I've heard it said that the first time it was uttered, it almost certainly was spoken with an Irish brogue. Celtic (*kel*-tik) Christians used the term as early as the fifth century. Where are your thin places? For me, it's the overstuffed chair in our family room. In the early morning light before anyone else awakens, I sit there most days with my Bible and a notebook. My morning ritual is to read from the *One Year Bible* and a devotional book and write my prayers in my journal, including prayers of adoration, confession, thanksgiving, and supplication.

I also love our back yard. Several years ago, we planted tropical floras that grow well in the California sunshine. On any given day, that scene can be a thin place. There is a walk in Kapalua, Maui, and another one in Cannon Beach, Oregon, that have become thin places for me. I also remember a time sitting quietly by myself in the garden of Gethsemane when I had a thin-place moment. Those are a few of my thin places. Obviously, you don't have to travel to exotic places or holy spots to find your thin place. It's more about searching for it and finding it often by surprise in a moment when your soul is invigorated. Reflect for a moment on where you find your thin places and consider what is special about them.

Use Your Gifts to Serve and Make a Difference

By the time you begin thinking about finishing well, you have finally become comfortable knowing what your gifts are and how you could make a difference in the world. Making a difference doesn't have to be a big thing, but people who finish well have learned to serve others. Writer and activist Parker Palmer says it so well: "No one has ever died saying, 'I'm so glad for the self-centered, self-serving, and self-protective life I lived.' Offer yourself to the world—your energies, your gifts, your visions, your spirit—with openhearted generosity."[27] What can you offer to make a difference?

Bob and Tanya volunteered to be premarital and marriage mentors to younger couples. Rachel decided it was time to put her money where her mouth is when it came to helping street kids in Kenya. As a single empty nester, she took time out of her busy schedule not only to give money but to help find donations for a wonderful organization that brings hope and healing to kids. When she had more time, she began taking women on "vision trips." She told me, "I'm just a mom with a heart for underserved kids." She has raised more than $20 million to erase poverty and bring hope to thousands of families, while juggling a career and keeping up with her adult children and grandchildren.

Obviously, not everyone is equipped or motivated to do what Rachel has done in Kenya. But everyone can make a difference serving others. Cathy makes cookies with her grandkids and passes them out to lonely neighbors. Bill volunteers on the coffee team at church. Cindy uses her resources and time to come alongside military families, showing love and appreciation to these heroes who often don't feel like heroes because their huge sacrifices go unnoticed. People who finish well know the joy of serving.

Nobel Peace Prize winner Albert Schweitzer summed it up this way: "I don't know what your destiny will be, but one thing I know: the only ones among you who will be really happy are those who will have sought and found how to serve."

The Life-Transforming Role of Mentoring

I'm deeply grateful for the many mentors in my life. While some might be surprised to know they helped mentor, influence, and guide me, others had a more direct or formal role in the shaping of who I am today. I met some of my most influential mentors after they had died—through their books. Now some of my mentors are younger than me. A mentor is an experienced and trusted advisor. Sometimes they are lifelong mentors, and other times they are with us for a season.

Lately, I've been trying to find the time to thank the people who have made a difference in my life. It has been a great exercise in the life-transforming role of mentoring. I'm convinced that anyone who achieves something significant has been inspired by a mentor along the way. Who are your mentors? Who has deeply affected your life? When I am speaking in a workshop, I sometimes ask people these questions. I'm always amazed how many times they say it was their mom or dad, or a grandparent, coach, teacher, or pastor. Seldom do the greatest influencers turn out to be famous. Rather, they're the people who saddled up next to them, believed in them, and pointed them in the right direction.

As you move toward the finish line, are you investing in others? In a healthy parent and adult child relationship, we get the chance to mentor our kids. It doesn't always come easily, but we can mentor our adult children when they invite us into their lives. We must remember that unsolicited advice is often taken as criticism and that waiting to be asked for our advice or influence can sometimes be difficult. But speaking from experience, I can tell you it's worth the wait. Are there others you can be influencing and mentoring? Someone at work, in your church, in your neighborhood? Just this weekend, a young couple we know well introduced us to two of their friends. They enthusiastically said, "Meet Jim and

Cathy. They are the mentors in our marriage that we told you about." Later, I asked Cathy if she knew we were mentors to them, and she smiled and said, "I had no idea." It gave us great joy to know that somewhere along the road, we had helped them. Here is what I have found over the years: when one person mentors, two lives are changed. As Parker Palmer writes, "Mentoring is a gift exchange in which we elders receive at least as much as we give, often more."[28] At the end of your life, few will talk about your material achievements. Rather, they'll talk about how your influence transformed others' lives.

Aging with Grace and Wisdom

You might not be there yet, but lately, I've thought about how weird it is to be the same age as old people. Now that I'm not only in the empty nest but also a grandparent, I reflect on my grandparents. I mean no offense to them, but they smelled a bit old and musty, just like their houses. As much as I loved them, they seemed just a bit out of touch. My experience is that those who embrace aging with grace and wisdom are the ones who finish well and make the biggest difference in the lives of those around them. And today you don't even need to smell musty. You can remain young at heart if you focus on what is beautiful and good. A person can age, but if their attitude is good, life can be good. A healthy attitude is more important than money or success. A positive attitude is a daily choice you can make. Your attitude is what will keep your influence from fading.

A few years ago, I rarely had conversations with my peers about aches and pains, but now I seldom have a conversation with peers that doesn't include a medical update. You may have a well-worn path from your bedroom to the bathroom because of all your trips there in the middle of the night, or you may have started to visit a specialist that you never knew existed. But the empty nest is no time to stop making a difference. Your experience is deeper and richer and more meaningful, and you can pass it on to younger generations. You have the privilege to pass on wisdom and inspiration. Finishing well means you aren't so much focused on rocking chairs and Metamucil as you are on giving of your life to make the world a better place. Preparation helps us finish the race well.

Chapter 8

EMPTY-NEST FRIENDSHIPS

Reach Out and Reconnect

❦

Principle 8: The keys to a happy life are strong friendships and a good support system.

❦

"I never thought my closest friends
would be those I found after fifty."

When I first started researching what life might look like in a healthy empty-nest season, I made a list of people I knew who appeared to have made the shift well, people who seemed to be thriving in the second half. I asked if I could interview them or if they would be willing to join a focus group to talk about their empty-nest experiences.

If I spoke to one hundred people, I received a hundred different answers and perspectives, but they all had one common denominator: quality friendships made a huge difference to their success. These people included introverts and extroverts, singles and married. Some of their adult kids were doing well, while others were struggling. It just kept coming back to quality friendships. I like how one woman put it: "My husband tells me I am a better wife and mother when I have spent time with friends who cause me to laugh or cry, accept me for who I am, and are my 'safe people.'"

One of the more outgoing people I know who had made the shift well wrote, "I love my book club, walking group, travel buddies, bridge group, work relationships, and one-on-one coffee times with friends. They've made me a better person and filled the void I had when my kids left." I'm an extrovert and her schedule makes even me tired. Another more introverted friend used the same phrase. "When our last child left the house, I *filled the void* with a weekly lunch with a friend from high school who was going through a similar experience." When I asked him about it, he said he reconnected with some of the deeper friendships that had slipped away because of his busy work and kid schedule. That was another word that kept coming up: reconnection.

The Friendship Factor

How are you doing with the friendship factor? Do you have a few deep friendships? Deep friendships are what I like to call replenishing relationships. You are blessed if you have deep friendships. More than 42 million Americans over the age of forty-five say that they suffer from chronic loneliness.[29] This statistic suggests that people are becoming disconnected, more isolated and lonelier, despite the worlds of Facebook, Instagram, and loads of other online connection tools. The study, conducted for the AARP and dubbed the "loneliness study," determined that loneliness is a significant predictor of poor health. Those who rated their health as excellent were less likely to be lonely than those who rated their health as poor (25 percent versus 55 percent).[30] Good friendships make a difference.

A Great Life Requires Great Friends

Because great friendships make a difference, we must be proactive. The empty nest is a time to focus on deepening connections with others. Most people unintentionally allow friendships to fade because of the high demands of family and work. What would a strong support network and social life look like for you? Proverbs 18:24 says, "One who has unreliable friends soon comes to ruin, but there is a friend who sticks closer than a brother [or sister]." As you look for deep, supportive friendships, remember they don't happen overnight. They are built over time as trust and vulnerability grow.

Friends accept you for who you are. Friends support and encourage you. Friends know your faults and love you anyway. They are caring and accepting. They tell you the truth, even if the truth hurts. Friends grieve with you, listen to you. They are willing to sacrifice for you. Friends are a safe place. Obviously, there are a limited number of people with all those attributes who can speak into our lives, but there is no reason not to find a few.

An old Russian proverb says, "Tell me who your friend is, and I will tell you who you are." My good friend Ted Cunningham likes to say, "The quality of your marriage depends a lot on the quality of your friends speaking into it. Marriage is a duet in need of great backup singers." Your investment in friendships is a determining factor in how you do life. Cathy and I are a part of a group of couples we call the BLAT Group. BLAT stands for Burns, Larsh, Alexander, and Toberty—the last names of these couples. This group has known each other for forty years. We have celebrated each other's weddings and the weddings of some of our children. We are together for significant events. We spent a week vacationing together in Hawaii. There have been highs and lows, sicknesses, joys, struggles, and through it all, the BLATs hang out and support one another. Cathy's and my marriage is richer and stronger because of them, and we are better parents because we've watched these beautiful people parent their own children. You don't need a group to hang with for forty years, but we all need friendships with people who will be there for us, and us for them.

How much time do you spend developing inspiring friendships and best-friends-forever relationships? It takes time and energy to develop those meaningful relationships, along with a willingness to sacrifice, but it's worth it. If you don't have great friendships, then don't despair. It's not too late to find friends who will encourage you and enrich your life, and for whom you will do the same. It's easiest with people who share your values. There is a great proverb that simply says, "Iron sharpens iron" (Prov. 27:17). When you share similar values, you tend to enhance each other's lives in deeper and more meaningful ways. My friend David started running with an acquaintance friend, Dana. After years of taking long runs together, their friendship blossomed into a close brother-to-brother relationship. Both men say they treasure their special friendship. The four men I've been having breakfast with for twenty years are closer than brothers in my life, and I am blessed by our relationships. When Jill's kids left the home, she reached out to her sister, who was in the same empty-nest season. Today, not only are they sisters but they are best friends. (Yes, it's possible in some families for siblings or cousins to be BFFs.) Whether it's going for a run together, sharing a meal, or two siblings reaching out, friendships often carry us through the empty-nest years.

Accountability and Confession

A deep friendship happens not only when you share fun and playfulness but also when you are vulnerable with each other. I like what John Townsend says in his book *How to Be a Best Friend Forever:* "Life is too short to go through it without vulnerability." He goes on to say, "We all need to be transparent about our inner selves, needs, mistakes, and emotions with someone. Best friends are the best place for that need."[31]

The safe place I have in my life is my men's breakfast group. It didn't begin that way. We started out talking about sports and politics and our shared faith. But when one of the guys opened up about a struggle he was having in his marriage, his vulnerability led to all of us becoming more open about our lives, doubts, struggles, family issues, and financial challenges. Today, that weekly Tuesday breakfast often is a thin place. What's amazing about thin places is that as much as they can be a sunset or a breathtaking look at nature, they are often when two or more friends share a meaningful connection. For me, those times happen when vulnerability is mixed with accountability and confession.

I remember as a young Christian reading a verse that confused me: "Therefore confess your sins to each other and pray for each other so that you may be healed" (James 5:16). Two things bothered me about that verse. I was not willing to confess my sins to anyone. I wanted to look good and put together. And sharing how I was missing the mark was just not in my DNA. I was trying to confess to God, but even that was a bit sketchy. But the part of that verse that bugged me the most was that if I confessed my sins to someone, I would be healed. That was just too much for me to fathom.

Then one day as a young Christian I took a risk and confessed to a mentor some things I had done and was going through. Instead of receiving wrath or rejection from this person, I received empathy and grace. He helped me to see I wasn't alone and helped me develop some accountability. That was the beginning of a truly beautiful healing process that made it easier to be more vulnerable in the future. That experience was my first encounter with a thin place, but it wasn't the last. Yes, honest, heartfelt confession in a trusted relationship can bring healing. It requires vulnerability, but it's worth the risk. I have learned over the years that private decisions, both good and bad, have public consequences. Confessing private decisions often brings wholeness to our lives.

The Value of Small Groups

When Wendy and Carl joined a couples' "life group" at their church, they had no idea it would become their lifeline.

Wendy was more excited than Carl about joining the group, meeting new friends, and building deeper community. Their last child had just moved out of the house, and Carl was focused on a recent promotion at work. Despite Carl's hesitancy, Wendy and Carl quickly found in the group deeper friendships and a sense of community they had not expected. Most of the couples were also recent empty nesters. Carl enjoyed conversations with the other men about sports, business, and travel, as well as the deeper connection and interaction around the study. He was new to most of the biblical teachings, but he felt very accepted, and the discussions were interesting and practical. The relationships with great people made the learning environment even better. Wendy couldn't get enough of her connection with several of the women in the small group and found she was scheduling coffee times with them and talking on the phone.

Then one day, they got the call no parent ever wants to get. Their young adult daughter had been in a terrible car crash near her university. Life changed that day for Carl and Wendy. I met them a year later. Their daughter was on a very long road to semirecovery, and all they could talk about was the incredible support they received from their small group. Carl told me, "It was our small group that carried us emotionally and spiritually through our toughest days, and we didn't even know them a year before our daughter's crash."

Judith, a recently divorced single mom, told me that the

secret to her sanity during her toughest days were three decisions she had made: to stay busy, to build friendships in her small group, and to make a difference in others' lives. Her small group of friends weekly volunteered to make a difference with an effort called Singles Against Cancer. Their common goal to fight cancer drew this small group of friends together in a big way.

Most of the time, you find powerful connection and community in a small group. Small groups create deeper friendships, produce maximum participation, provide flexible learning experiences, and for many people, form a sort of extended family. Cathy and I are huge believers in small groups. Here is our list of benefits: community, connection, opportunities to give and receive advice, encouragement, deeper and more flexible experiential learning, fun, networking, role models, deeper friendships, and extended family. If it sounds like I'm trying to sell you on joining a small group that works for you, I am.

It wasn't that long ago that people grew up in villages and small towns. For good and for bad, the small town or village was a source of community and connection. As people moved away from their villages, later in life they realized they still needed one. No one needs to go through the empty-nest season alone. Is it time for you to recreate your village?

Chapter 9

SINGLE PARENT, EMPTY NEST

Principle 9: Let go even when you want to hold on.

*"Even though I felt totally alone, I
knew there were millions of other single
parents who had gone before me and
come out better on the other side."*

One of Cathy's and my very good friends is a single mom
whose last child was about to leave home for college. We
admire this woman greatly as a wonderful parent who sacri-
ficed so much for her family, juggled her job, and poured her
life into her kids. I asked her if she was ready for the empty
nest. Her short answer was, "Sure," sounding anything but.
She then broke down sobbing and said, "Are you kidding

me? I'm not, and I'm scared of the quiet and emptiness that await my life." She added, "I know it's best for him, but this is not easy." To some extent hers is the cry of many empty nesters, but for most single parents, it's an even more intense challenge. The empty-nest syndrome often hits single parents significantly harder. Much of what has been written about the empty nest identifies this time as an opportunity for spouses to reconnect but largely ignores the challenges facing single parents.

My experience with single parents is that they usually do a great job raising their kids but are often too busy or distracted to celebrate a job well done. Single parents make countless sacrifices for their children and their families. They typically can't indulge in a few hours of leisure or sneak away for "me time" while the other parent takes over. Married parents can lean on each other when the kids leave home. They have someone who understands to share their feelings with. But single parents don't have that shared experience. One person put it this way: "As a single parent, I think I had a bit of a different kind of relationship with my kids than some of the two-parent families I know. From the time of the divorce, we formed a tight bond and had to rely more heavily on each other. In positive and sometimes not so positive ways, we became enmeshed with our decisions and support for one another that felt different when I was still married." Out of necessity, many single parents learn to be strong and resilient and find they need to rely more heavily on their friends and family. All parents make sacrifices, but as a single parent, your needs take a back seat to the more pressing needs of your family, perhaps for years. No one ever said this empty-nest phase would be easy. And it's not.

The Challenges

Two Huge Upheavals

Carol Brzozowski, a single mom going through the empty nest, nailed it when she wrote, "For the single-parent empty nester, life has presented at least two major upheavals, divorce from or death of a spouse and the bittersweet day when the last child leaves home."[32] For many people, grief after divorce or the death of a spouse runs jagged and deep. The grief of entering the empty nest is similar for single parents. Just like moving from a two-parent household to a one-parent household can be a shock to the system, so it is when you move from having a teenager living in the home, with all their energy, spontaneity, drama, and fun, to a home where everything is profoundly quiet and empty. A friend of mine told me after her daughter moved out of the house, "It feels vacant, almost uninhabited." She said, "The quietness is shouting every time I walk into the house as the memories keep flooding in." She didn't like the feeling, and I think she was talking not only about her daughter's departure but about her own transition as well.

Transition Is Hard

Transition can be a bumpy ride for anyone. The transition to the empty nest isn't just about being confronted with quietness in the home. It might be more about your identity. When our kids were home, one result of all of their extracurricular activities, including school functions and church parties at our house, was that I became very comfortable being known as Christy, Rebecca, and Heidi's dad. I was identified by my role in my kids' lives. Many of my friendships and conversations took place at games and dance recitals. It happened so quickly: after years of constant activity, the events abruptly stopped. And I realized that I had lost a significant number of spontaneous relationships. It was lonely.

In the transition, be aware that you may experience symptoms of depression or anxiety in your adjustment to your children being gone. For me, these symptoms were triggered by the sight of an empty room or a vacant spot at the table. I missed our special dates for fun food or walks on the beach. As the memories flooded in, it was brutal. The move from actively parenting to not being needed daily hit me hard. Change is difficult for me anyway. I've lived in the same house and worked at the same job most of my adult life. My guess is most dedicated single parents find it especially challenging.

Even the mildest symptoms of anxiety and depression are your body and mind signaling your discomfort. If you are experiencing any of these transition responses, know that what you are going through is normal and emotionally draining. There really isn't a right way to feel. Most parents vacillate between sadness and joy.

Empty House, Empty Bank Account

Some single parents have the misconception that when the last child leaves home, there will be a bit more money in the bank. The following is one woman's story, but I repeatedly hear stories just like it when I speak on the empty-nest years. Diane is a single mom who had two adult children moving out at about the same time. "As much as I was excited about my two kids going to college, I knew child support was ending—not that my ex ever really took that court mandate as seriously as I had hoped or expected. Most of the financial load was on me. Then my ex and I had 'the talk' about helping with college expenses. That did not go well. He refused to pay a dime. My mom chipped in some, I started working a second job, my kids paid some, and I borrowed more to make it work. The empty bank account just made it more clear to me that my marriage had failed and now I was reaping the 'benefit' of an unsupportive ex who had already married and had another baby and a life outside of our family. My general feeling was anger at him and anger at myself. It wasn't a good season of life for me, and it just added to the loss I was feeling from my kids' departure into adulthood."

Diane learned two lessons about finances and the empty nest:

1. **You can't please everyone all the time.** She found herself getting deeper and deeper into debt to help her kids, and she knew that was not going to play out well for her future. Many adult children have figured out how to go through college without their parents' financial support. Trying to please everyone is a recipe for stress, misery, and frustration. As a recovering people pleaser who has fallen off the wagon hundreds of times, I keep this saying close to my heart: "No matter how hard I try, I can never please everyone." I once heard someone say, "I don't know the secret to success for a family, but I do know the secret to failure: trying to keep everyone happy all the time."

2. **Don't be afraid to talk about money with your adult kids.** Not wanting to throw her ex under the bus, Diane didn't talk about her financial struggles with her adult children. She felt she would be burdening them if she shared her challenges. The lesson she learned was that her kids truly *did* want to know, and they wanted to be part of the solution. Her kids were willing to do whatever it took to get to college, and they let their mom know that fact only after she

confided in them. This is not always the situation, but they also went to their dad and ended up getting a little help from him as well.

Embrace the New Normal

This thought by Haim Ginott, one of the true pioneers in the field of parenting, helped me greatly with the empty nest: "This could be your finest hour. To let go when you want to hold on requires utmost generosity and love. Only parents are capable of such painful greatness."

As your kids leave home, you really have only two options: panic and stay stuck, or move forward and reframe your life. Brzozowski outlines the dilemma in her own life: "It's the great paradox of having achieved what you have worked for years to accomplish: teaching your child to be independent and then mourning the time when they actually do take the reins."[33] When their children move away, single parents usually have more time. Though that can mean more time and energy to do things you enjoy, it may also mean that you have just had a major source of your purpose and joy removed. It's time to acknowledge that much of your life revolved around the kids, and now, not only are you letting go because it's right for them, but also you are preparing for a new phase in your life. Good thing this doesn't happen in one day. It's a process that usually takes years. The ones who do it best acknowledge that they need to find and embrace a new normal. And one size does not fit all.

Moving Forward

What does moving forward look like? Let's talk about five different steps in this process.

1. Remember that your children haven't left your life. Your role is changing, but don't forget that an adult-to-adult parenting relationship can have major benefits. It's easy to forget that our teenagers were both absolute angels and completely awful from time to time while they were working on their own identity. Your adult children no longer live under your roof, but that doesn't mean you can't reinvent the relationship for the better. You can look forward to a new chapter with them.

2. As you reinvent the relationship, avoid leaning on your adult children for emotional support. In a single-parent home, an incredible parent-child emotional bond often takes place. A single parent helped me understand this when she said, "At the time of the divorce, the relationship with my kids shifted and we formed our own tight clan. In subtle ways, we became our own support system." She was explaining this to me as she told me how difficult but good it was to learn not to depend on them as she once had. It's not good to depend on your adult children for your emotional support. If you don't have a support system outside of your kids, it's time to make sure you find one. It's a way of respecting the new relationship with your kids and is much better for you in the long run. Here is a good principle to remember and live by: if you lean too hard, you will push them away.

3. Work out flexible ways to stay in touch. Let your child set the pace, but make sure you are planning fun and meaningful events without intruding on their newfound freedom. When our daughter Becca went away to college, I had dinner with her almost every Tuesday night. Sometimes it was just with Becca, and other times it was with a group of her friends. She lived about an hour away, and I usually spent more time driving than eating, but it was worth it. Some of my best conversations with Becca happened during those "spontaneous" meals. About the time our kids moved out, we began to offer them annual family trips that were such fun, they were almost too hard not to accept: anything from a beach vacation to staying in a friend's cabin in the mountains. They all show up for at least part of the time. What can you do to make something happen? It doesn't have to be expensive. It does need to be as fun and drama free as possible. Building new family traditions can be fun and enjoyable. As your children transition to adulthood, it's time to focus less on the ending (the empty nest) and more on the beginning—the future, which is wide open.

4. Reactivate your social life. If you're like many single parents, you invested much of your time, talent, and treasure in your kids while they were living at home. Now that you have more free time, invest in your own social life. For most people, replenishing relationships and deeper friendships don't just show up at the door. You have to make them happen. So if you need to get back in the game of having a social life and developing meaningful friendships, this is your time to shine. This is a bit easier for the extrovert than the introvert. But the good news is that an introvert probably needs less social stimulation and can be comfortable with a few good friends.

We discussed friendships in the previous chapter, but let me meddle a bit on the question of whether to date. Ultimately, the decision to date or remarry is yours only, even though friends and family undoubtedly will have an opinion. If they are like most friends and family, they won't be shy about offering their opinions. But realize that you and you alone should decide. Their intentions are probably good, though, and who knows, they might have some worthy advice for you. With that in mind, since you've read this far in the book, consider yourself my friend and hear a couple of my thoughts:

1. Don't let loneliness catapult you into the wrong relationship. Though the nest is quiet and you are feeling alone, an unhealthy or dysfunctional relationship will not fill that void. It will only complicate it. A high-profile Christian leader once told me, "I was in a poor marriage where my husband cheated on me for most of our twenty-seven years of marriage. After my divorce and the kids moved out, I immediately ran into the arms of a man my friends and parents warned me about. They begged me to take it slow. I didn't heed their advice, and we were married within two months of meeting each other. Six months later, I fled this abusive relationship and was even more unhappy." The lesson here is don't run to a relationship to fill a void. You don't need to be in a romantic relationship to be a whole person.

2. Do the premarital work. Here is a phenomenal fact: for those willing to invest in premarital education and counseling, the odds that they will divorce is 31 percent lower.[34] When my friend Doug Fields and I wrote the book and workbook *Getting Ready for Marriage*, we were surprised that many people getting remarried weren't open to getting premarital counseling or even reading a book. I believe that fact has a direct correlation to the poor success of remarriages. It doesn't have to be that way.

Jay and Leesa are great people who came to my office to discuss getting married. Both were in their midfifties and divorced, and their kids were emerging adults. They had met at church, and because both had come from less than perfect marriages, they didn't want to make the same mistakes. In the first meeting, I gave them a worksheet titled Five Crucial Questions created by Doug Fields and me in our book, *Getting Ready for Marriage*.[35] Here are those questions:

1. **Are you willing to work at premarital education?** With the divorce rate so high among empty-nest marriages, working toward a 31 percent better chance of success is of utmost importance. I consider it a red flag if even one member of the couple isn't willing to do the work before getting married.

2. **Are you willing to hear from your relational community?** Sometimes those who love you and believe in you see things that you don't see. Take the temperature of your friends and family.

3. **Are you willing to look for red flags?** If a couple is unwilling to identify and take seriously some red flags, that raises a red flag for *me*. Here is just a short list: addiction, abuse, unfaithfulness, community concern, sexual activity, differing spiritual values, poor communication and conflict-resolution skills, major unresolved issues with a previous spouse or adult children. What advice would you give your adult children if their significant other had some of those red flags? I'm sure you would tell them to get help before jumping into that relationship.

4. **Are you willing to be brutally honest about your brokenness?** If you are not happy being single and you have some major issues in your life, don't believe that a new marriage will fix your problems. No one is

perfect, and everyone has been hurt, but work through your brokenness before the wedding, not after.

5. **Are you ready for unconditional commitment?** As you already know, getting married is one of the most important decisions of your life. If you are not willing to promise faithfulness, perseverance, loyalty, and commitment, then you aren't ready for marriage.

Jay and Leesa's answers confirmed they had done the work and were ready for remarriage, and today their marriage and blended family are models for others.

5. Practice healthy doses of self-care. When kids are living at home, most single parents are so busy they often put off the important work of self-care. I love what American author Carlos Castaneda once said: "We either make ourselves miserable or we make ourselves strong. The amount of work is the same." Self-care is not self-indulgence or selfishness. And there is no one-size-fits-all strategy. Part of your second-half makeover is to look at your physical, social, mental, emotional, and spiritual self-care and make yourself strong instead of miserable. How would that look for you?

You need to find what works for you. Kathleen put extra energy and time into nurturing her spiritual life. She told me that when the kids were living at home, she neglected her soul care. Gerald found it difficult to seek the support of others, but he decided it was time to include some friends and family in this new phase of life. Others have mentioned to me that seeking counseling or coaching had profound results, or that joining a small group of like-minded people was helpful. One woman I know shared in a focus group, "I was divorced when the kids were in high school and was too busy to dig up the scars then. I put it off, but the ghosts of past relationships were still in my life. I didn't get help and healing until I put time and energy into working on it."

For others, as they entered a healthy self-care stage, they learned that maintaining a separate identity from being a parent was critical to their lives. Most set new goals, including time to rest, relax, and rejuvenate. For one person, bringing home a rescue from the dog pound was key to her self-care. She said, "Today it's just me and the dog. That dog is my constant companion, and I'm never really lonely." As I mentioned, self-care is not one size fits all. What will it take for you to get emotionally, physically, and spiritually healthy for this next phase? My guess is you know the answer.

I wish you could meet our special friend Connie. She is a single parent who lives in the empty nest with her dog, Fido—honestly, the dog's name is Fido. She embodies a lot of the healthy thoughts I share in this chapter. Her children are active in her life, but she doesn't depend on them to bring her happiness. They bring her lots of joy and undoubtedly a few concerns, but she knows she also had to reinvent her relationship with them and develop a new strategy in the second half of life. Today she is busy with work, friendships, volunteering, her church, and spending adult-to-adult time with her kids either in person or online. Connie has taught my wife and me so much about living a healthy, vibrant lifestyle throughout whatever life throws your way. She has taught us that in the second half, we need to slow down and enjoy our lives. We need to stop and have some serious fun, to take more time to enjoy nature and to nurture our friendships and our spiritual lives. It's out of our greater appreciation for the life God has given us that, as Anne Lamott likes to say, "we can begin to give in wildly generous ways to the world out of our abundance." We've learned from Connie that the quicker we make healthy changes, the better it gets. Never perfect, but better. The more time I spent researching and talking to single parents in the empty nest, the more parents I found like Connie, both male and female, who have chosen to fill their lives with good things. You can too.

More Ideas for Self-Care

1. Volunteer.
2. Mentor someone.
3. Work with children.
4. Connect with other singles and marrieds in specialized groups.

5. Be proactive about connecting with friends and family.
6. Join support groups for empty-nest singles.
7. Start a hobby or renew an old one.
8. Get a job or change jobs.
9. Find a coach or counselor.
10. Stay positive.
11. Start a bucket list.
12. Schedule ongoing weekly relational times with a group.
13. Get a pet.
14. Refresh your resume.
15. Add comedy to your life.
16. Learn a new skill.
17. Exercise and get in shape.
18. Take some courses or go back to school.
19. Take up kayaking, walking, or any exercise that gets you outdoors.
20. Pursue your passions.
21. Channel your emotions with good things:

- journaling
- creativity
- drawing
- painting
- decorating
- serving
- church work
- international trips

Now you add to this list what ideas would work for you.

_____

Chapter 10

HOW TO BE THE GROOVIEST GRANDPARENT IN TOWN

Principle 10: Your greatest impact just might be with your grandchildren.

"Now that I have grandchildren, this is my priority! It's a marvelous love affair between generations."

Just today as I began writing this chapter on grandparenting, I looked up at the clock and realized I had volunteered to pick up our grandson James from preschool at noon. It was almost time to pick him up, but I was on a roll with my writing. The car seat was in my car, and Cathy was watching Charlotte, our three-year-old granddaughter, and Huxley, our six-month-old grandson. It was a full day of grandparenting and out of the question to bail on the pickup. I found myself in the familiar old rush of young parents.

At the school, the line was long and chaotic and the parking lot was a mess. I got out of my car, and suddenly, I saw my grandson jumping up and down and yelling to all his friends, "Yay! Yay! My Papa J is here! My Papa J is here!" Then he pointed at me and, with great energy, shouted, "That's my Papa J!" He jumped out of the waiting area before he was really supposed to and came running into my arms. I'm so glad I was wearing sunglasses, because my eyes were filled with tears of joy.

The love affair between a grandparent and a grandchild is beyond description. I instantly lost all interest in my writing and other responsibilities and just wanted to spend as much time as possible with my little five-year-old buddy. I am quite aware that he will reach an age when his unbounding enthusiasm for me will diminish. But this I know: I have a shot at building a legacy of love with these grandchildren of mine as I make them a top priority for my life. I've never felt unconditional love and overwhelming acceptance from another human like I have from my grandchildren. I want them to feel the same from me.

A Legacy of Love

How about you? How will you build a legacy of love with your grandchildren? I'm always amazed how many times people tell me, "It was the strength and prayers and influence of my grandma [or grandpa] that got me through the trials of my life." Parents influence kids the most, but grandparents, according to research, are right behind. Life is generational, and for me, having grandkids has helped me understand that my greatest impact just might be with the next generations. One of the major themes of the Bible is "from generation to generation." With grandchildren, we can have a marvelous love affair between generations. My friends Tim and Darcy Kimmel write in their excellent book *Extreme Grandparenting*, "Some people will misunderstand the term 'empty nest' as freedom from responsibility for their offspring." No way. "Grandparenting offers us a chance to groom a generation for greatness."[36] That sounds like a much better investment of our lives than watching old reruns of *I Love Lucy* or the Golf Channel.

As grandchildren began arriving in their family, our friend Susan told her husband, Randy, "Now that I have grandchildren, this is my priority." Randy told me recently that the number-one ministry involvement they have is their grandchildren. As I have mentioned, my wife, Cathy, retired from teaching to be a fully engaged grandma. Most people can't totally stop what they are doing, but they can move around some other priorities to include the high calling of being a grandparent. This even goes for those who are having the heartwrenching experience of grandparenting from a distance because their kids and grandkids don't live nearby. Here is a great truth to live by: "The best thing to spend on your grandkids is time." It may be quality time snuggling up next to your granddaughter as I did yesterday with Charlotte, making up a story about Princess Charlotte, or it may be FaceTiming with your grandson after his big game. Time matters and makes a difference.

I wrote about my grandma Nene in *Doing Life with Your Adult Children*. I'm sure she never read a book or attended a class on grandparenting, but she was just an incredibly wonderful grandma. She didn't have a lot of money for fancy trips or expensive gifts, but she knew how to focus all her attention on us grandkids. She attended our games. She created a party out of everything. We called her and my mom "the party time grandma." Grandma Nene instinctively knew what it means to build lifelong memories and traditions. When we were in her presence, she gave us her devotion. I'm sure every one of my brothers and I thought we were her favorite. I'm sure she had never heard of the term, but she was a natural at "positive spoiling." And we would have done anything for that beautiful woman. Even last night, as two of our grandchildren had a sleepover with us, I thought of my own grandma. I put aside whatever I was going to do and just hung out with them.

Your influence is not going to come from the money you leave your grandkids after you die or the things you give them. What will stick with them forever is the atmosphere of love mixed with grace, joy, fun, laughter, and affection that you create for them. What does your home *feel* like to your grandkids? Many of us grew up visiting our grandparents' homes, and they felt musty, formal, and stiff. But today you can focus on building a welcoming atmosphere of fun food, games, laughter, traditions, and even spiritual blessings.

My mom had a bottom drawer that was always filled with surprises for my kids. They would run into the house, and sometimes even before greeting Grandma and Grandpa, they would head to the drawer, never to be disappointed. She would have just baked cookies, and the smell would still be filling the home. Total confession: that's where I usually headed. Nothing like those chocolate-chip cookies. It was as if my mom and dad were just waiting for us to show up. And they probably were, but that kind of welcoming spirit is what we all want to create for our grandkids. I wish I could show you a photo of my wife's office. She has a beautiful desk, a computer, files, and all the important things it takes to run our finances, our home, and her life. But the other half of her office has a large children's play kitchenette, books, stuffed animals, art projects, blocks, cars, and Legos, and the last time I looked, it even had a children's shopping cart in the corner. Whatever the age of your grandkids may be, what can you do to ensure they sense, "You are welcome here"?

What Can I Do to Help?

There is an African proverb that became a political statement, but it rings true for our role as grandparents: "It takes a village to raise a child." Children need more than just Mom and Dad's influence. They need our relationship. Our job is never to replace their parents but rather to come alongside their parents whenever we can to help them and be their chief cheerleaders.[37] Even when our kids aren't raising our grandchildren exactly how we would do it, our job is to help, not to interfere. Only in cases of abuse and endangerment should we intervene.

Availability to your kids and grandkids is a huge thing. I'm sure you remember how difficult it was to juggle parenting and life. Now you have the chance, if you live nearby, to say, "How can I help?" You can ask, "Can we watch the kids while you go on a date?" Or, "How about if we take the kids overnight so you can have some time together?" Then make that overnighter a total party time for the kids, no matter what the age. Helping to carry the burden of parenting by giving our children some occasional relief is a perfect way to continue our legacy of love. And the benefit is we get to give those grandkids back so we can rest. One woman told me, "My grandkids think I am the oldest person in the world, and after watching them for a weekend while their parents were away, I think they are right." This just may be your greatest legacy, and it starts with some good ol' availability and party time.

The Blessing

For years, whenever I heard someone refer to "the blessing," I thought it might be some weird ritual. I know that Old Testament patriarchs on their deathbeds often offered a special blessing to their children and grandchildren. I don't think we grandparents have to wait for the deathbed to do it. I think bringing security and honor to our grandkids by showering them with blessings is a natural part of what it means to be a grandparent and to keep the positive legacy alive by passing it from generation to generation. The Kimmels say that every child is born with three key needs:

1. A secure love
2. A significant purpose
3. A sufficient hope[38]

Often the best thing for a child who is compromising their values and longing for acceptance is to have a grandparent believe in them and accept them with unconditional love. The biblical blessing is the greatest way to bring out the best in our grandkids. Children typically struggle in the absence of the blessing of love, affirmation, belief, and celebration. When this blessing is withheld, unmet needs for security and acceptance eat away at the core of their lives. It's quite possible you never had a sense of blessing from your parents, but your kids and grandkids can know an incredible sense of security and honor. Here are four ways you can influence your grandchildren by offering blessings to them.

1. Speak the Blessing

Your words have great power with your grandchildren. Your tongue can bless your grandkids with words of affirmation and strength. The writer of the book of Proverbs says, "The tongue has the power of life and death" (Prov. 18:21). You can speak words of life to your grandkids that can transform them. Your words of blessing can heal wounds. At the end of her life, my mom's last words to me were, "Jimmy, I love you, and I'm proud of you." I will gratefully live with that blessing for the rest of my life. When you liberally praise your children and your children's children, you give them a gift that is beyond measure.

2. Believe the Blessing

The power of *showing* belief in your grandchildren and your adult children may be more important than just using words. Don't forget that the difference between kids who make it and kids who don't is often just one caring adult. A young person's identity and self-image are wrapped up not only in what they believe about themselves but also in how others view them. Even when a child has strayed from your values and made poor choices, one of the major questions they are quietly asking is, "Do you still love me?"

A friend of mine who grew up with a speech impediment and learning challenges had a grandfather who was the constant in his life and kept believing in him. His grandfather would ask, "What are your dreams?" And then the grandfather would say, "I believe you can do that. You have the power within yourself, and you are a child of God." Today that friend is a well-known psychologist who helps kids with learning issues thrive. Authorities tell us that the healthiest and most successful kids are the ones who have someone believing in them and cheering them on.

3. Be the Blessing

You are a role model to your grandchildren. When they are young, they will imitate your behaviors, and as they grow older, they will take on some of your values. Life is messy, and sometimes, just like us, kids will wander from the path, but one of the most effective ways to bring them back is through your modeling integrity. There is great truth in this proverb: "Whoever walks in integrity walks securely" (Prov. 10:9). If you walk with integrity, you will be more secure, and likewise your grandkids will experience more security as well. When you realize you are a role model, you are a step closer to understanding that a part of your job description as a grandparent is to find ways to mentor your grandchildren. It comes as a surprise to many grandparents that, after parents, grandparents have the most influence on kids' lives, but it's time to embrace that fact and be a mentor to your grandkids.

When you are being a mentor and a role model, you are leaving clear tracks for your grandkids to follow. When I was young, my parents and my grandma would take me to the beach to play in the sand and swim. As we walked along the edge of the ocean, I would put my feet inside my parents' and grandma's footprints. It was a fun game, but later I realized it was a strong metaphor for following the way of my parents and grandma. We don't have to be perfect to be a blessing. Kids understand that we all miss the mark. What they want is someone to be a leader in their lives, an authentic leader they can follow. That sounds like a sacred and grand calling for any grandparent.

4. Celebrate the Blessing

My mother had a wonderful philosophy: celebrate everything. And of course, with this kind of attitude she was the favorite grandma, the favorite mother-in-law, the favorite friend. Part of giving your grandkids a blessing is celebrating their milestones and rites of passage. Just show up and be ready to have fun. Many other cultures do a more effective job than ours at celebrating rites of passage and milestones. In our home, we make birthdays a big thing. We always celebrate with a terrific, fun meal, and then we play a game of "affirmation bombardment," where each family member says three good and affirming things about the birthday person. It's fun, meaningful, sometimes emotional, and always well received. It turns out to be a huge blessing.

My friend Jeremy Lee and I wrote a book called *Pass It On*,[39] in which we give parents and grandparents ideas to celebrate various rites of passage for kids from kindergarten through high school graduation. You can use it to cheer your grandchildren on and bless them by being present, either in person or digitally, for any milestone—graduating from a grade, getting a driver's license, and even reaching puberty. Yes, I know a family who actually celebrated puberty with each of their kids. That might sound strange, but it's not just about body changes but about entering a new phase of life. When our girls were eleven years old, Cathy took each one on an overnight trip, bought them an outfit, had a fun meal, and then read a short book with them about changes that were taking place in their bodies and in their relationships. When they turned sixteen, I was their first date, and we had a similar experience. These were markers in their lives that made lifelong positive memories. Grandparents can do the same types of things. James and I are planning our first trip to one of my speaking engagements. Charlotte and I have a date this summer for a day trip to an amusement park. These experiences make forever memories, and your grandkids will later look at them as blessings in their lives.

As you can see, a blessing for your grandkids can come in all types of forms. When you bless your grandchildren, you bring happiness to them by, in one way or another, invoking God's favor on them. A blessing is a gift of your time, energy, wisdom, and resources to shower them with your love and the love of God. For me, the exercise of bestowing blessings on my grandchildren has a spiritual dynamic. It's passing on the legacy of faith from generation to generation. This is one of my major goals. How about you?

> Since my youth, God, you have taught me,
>> and to this day I declare your marvelous
>>> deeds.
> Even when I am old and gray,
>> do not forsake me, my God,
> till I declare your power to the next
>> generation,
>>> your mighty acts to all who are to come.
>
> —PSALM 71:17–18

Grandparenting through the Tough Times

Loving our children's children can also bring heartache or pain. Larry Fowler puts it so well in his book *Overcoming Grandparenting Barriers*: "The deeper the relationship, the greater the joy—or the pain—it can bring."[40] Many grandparents feel at a loss to help when there is geographical distance or when dealing with a crisis because of their children's or grandchildren's poor choices and broken relationships, but these are perfect times to come alongside and be present in their lives.

Ben and Barbara sat with me over coffee after I gave a seminar on the empty nest at their church. They were in great anguish over their adult daughter's poor choices and the effect of those choices on their two grandchildren. I didn't give them easy answers or platitudes. There are none that would have helped. Their daughter had strayed far from their values and faith. She had made one bad decision after another. Drugs, lost faith, a divorce, major blended-family issues, and separation from the family were all part of what they were experiencing. They were filled with worry and regrets even in their own lives. "What did we do wrong?"

This I know: good parents and grandparents can still have kids and grandkids who make poor choices. Here is what we came up with in that conversation. No matter what happens, they could be a safe place for their daughter and her kids. Ben and Barb could offer grace and love, even as they were grieving poor decisions. It is possible to be a safe place even when you are offering tough love. Tough love is simply showing love while allowing the natural consequences of poor choices to play out. Sometimes the best thing to do is not to bail them out but to be there for emotional support. When our children or grandchildren make unwise decisions, life is fluid, but as we create a safe place of love for them, when they fall, they will return to that safe place. If we choose meanness, shunning, or anger, they will look for help somewhere else when they fall.

We also had to talk about these parents' deep regrets and their second-guessing about their parenting and family. They kept questioning, "What could we have done to keep them from poor choices?" I heard a lot of couldas and shouldas. Everyone lives with regrets. It's how we handle our regrets that makes a huge difference in our lives. I love what former secretary of state Colin Powell once said in an interview: "What good are regrets? Regrets slow you down. Regrets cause you to fail to pay attention to the future. So I never log, count, or inventory my regrets. I move on."[41] That's good advice, though it's not always easy to follow. We can't just bury our regrets. The best thing to do with them is to name them, apologize for them when needed, practice gratitude for what we have, be compassionate toward ourselves, not taking too much credit for someone else's poor choices, learning from them, and moving forward. For me it's a spiritual discipline found in the writing of the apostle Paul: "I have not achieved it, but I focus on this one thing: Forgetting the past and looking forward to what lies ahead, I press on to reach the end of the race and receive the heavenly prize for which God, through Christ Jesus, is calling us" (Phil. 3:13–14 NLT).

Long-Distance Grandparenting

Words cannot adequately express the joy grandkids bring us and the sadness we so often feel when they live far away from us. When we experience what my friend Wayne Rice calls the "distance dilemma," it does take more time, energy, and creativity to stay close with our grandkids. He also says distance can provide an opportunity to be "intentional about connecting with grandchildren and doing so with regularity."[42] Some grandparents take proximity for granted and miss great opportunities for connection.

Because we live in a digital age, it's easier than ever to stay connected. This new generation of kids uses the internet, social media, FaceTime, texting, and whatever the latest form of communication is to stay connected with their friends, so it's time for grandparents to brush up on their media skills and keep connected. If it feels strange to you, it doesn't to them. It's their normal. Many of the experiences in the ideas section of this chapter work for long distance just as well as if your grandkids live around the corner.

No, the empty nest, as good as it can be, is not the time to step away from the responsibility and privilege of impacting another generation. Just the opposite. The empty nest gives you the opportunity to focus on passing your values on to the next generations. Long after you are gone from earth, your legacy will continue from generation to generation. Just this morning I was sitting in my chair in my thin place. I had done some reading and drunk some coffee and was waiting for two of my grandchildren to wake up. I then heard the pitter-patter of their feet running around, and finally they came bouncing downstairs already full of energy and life. They both came and jumped on my lap. They asked if they could watch the children's Bible app on my phone. Together we watched a fun episode about David and Goliath. Then Charlotte, age three, looked up at me, put her little hand on my cheek, and said, "Papa J, you are my best friend." In that moment, I knew all was right with the world and that I would invest the rest of my life in those little best friends of mine, coming alongside to bless them, encourage them, and help them on their way.

I've never met a single grandparent who said that putting time and energy into their relationships with their grandchildren was not worth it. This seems to be the part of our legacy in the empty nest that we can most easily understand.

Yes, your greatest influence with those grandkids may come after you have passed into eternity. You don't have to be cool to make an eternal difference. You don't even have to live in the same town. Nobody said it would always be easy, and some families find it's more complicated than others, but your love affair with your grandkids gives you influence from generation to generation.

Practical Connection Ideas

1. **Vacation together.** If you can, get away together once a year. Make it simple for your adult kids and grandkids. If the adult kids can't come, invite the grandkids.

2. **Make Sunday family time.** Some families have something like an open house for the family on Sunday nights. Have some fun food or a potluck.

3. **Start a cousins' camp.** How about establishing a yearly "cousins' camp"? Invite all your grandchildren over for a weekend. Fun is what the weekend is all about. Play together and eat fun food. Spoil them. Allow them to interact with each other and send them home happy. Then take a nap.

4. **Take a grandparents' trip.** What about taking a rite of passage trip? At a certain age, take each grandchild on a vacation and let them help plan the trip. Just this one grandchild. It'll create a lifelong memory.

5. **Make your home grandchild friendly.** Have favorite foods for them when they come over. Depending on their age, have some special toys at your house just for them. A grandma's drawer full of fun things to do is a good idea. Know what their favorite shows are and sit down and watch them together. Maybe have some popcorn or other fun food. Have a tea party.

6. **Create a grandkids' fund.** Maybe you can help with camp or school or a college savings plan. Help them pay for a missions trip. Grandkids are a great investment.

7. **Do projects together.** Bake and cook together. Create photo albums, digital or old school. Play a continuous game together. Do some crafts. How about starting a family history project?

8. **Take them to church.** Take them to church with you when you can. Stop by a donut shop before or after. Let them know you pray for them regularly. Get them one of the many Bible apps for watching age-appropriate shows on the phone, iPad, or computer.

9. **Use digital devices to connect.** Keep in touch with your grandkids with email, FaceTime, Zoom, phone calls, and texts. Share photos with each other. Send them inspirational YouTube videos. Watch a movie together in different homes. Share jokes. Join an online sports fantasy league together.

QUESTIONS FOR REFLECTION

Chapter 1: Empty or Full? Challenge or Opportunity?

1. If you've taken the Empty-Nest Syndrome Quiz (pp. 12–13), how did you feel about the questions? Do you wish to change any of your answers?

2. What is the best part of your transition to the empty nest?

3. What is the most difficult part of your transition to the empty nest?

4. How does the quote at the start of the chapter relate to you personally? "I miss their mess. I miss their noise. I miss their rudeness and neediness. I miss their laughter. I miss my place in their lives. Who am I, and what do I do with the rest of my life?"

5. Consider the following four important steps toward a fresh start. Which do you need to work on?

    a. Close the chapter.

    b. Choose to change your attitude and perspective.

    c. Set new personal goals.

    d. Make new friends and enhance old friendships.

Chapter 2: Reinventing the Relationship with Your Adult Children

1. On a scale of 1 to 5, with 1 being "needs major improvement" and 5 being "excellent," how would you rate your relationship with your adult children? Why did you choose that number?

2. Do you have difficulty expressing expectations to your adult children? Reconsider the five big questions. Which are going well for you, and which need improvement?

   a. Have you relinquished control and given your adult children the passport to adulthood?

   b. Are you enabling dependency?

   c. Do you want it more than they want it?

   d. Are you communicating with them on an adult-to-adult level?

   e. Are you ready for the boomerang?

3. Do you believe you have adequately expressed your expectations to your adult children regarding issues that are important to you?

4. Money can have a high cost on your relationship. Do you believe you have done what is needed to uncomplicate it and create an environment that equips your adult children to be financially responsible, or do you need more work in this area?

Chapter 3: Reinventing Yourself for the Rest of Your Life

1. The empty nest is a rite of passage for you. What one course correction would help you embrace positive change in this time of your life?
2. Is there an area of self-care you could focus on, keeping in mind that small changes equal amazing new outcomes?
3. Peter Drucker said, "First things first, last things not at all." What in your life is weighing you down and could use some decluttering? What would it take to declutter that part of your life? What's holding you back?
4. Do you have a dream-on list? If not, spend a few moments creating a short one. What is on that list that you would really like to do or experience?
5. Look at the sidebar on the benefits of the empty nest (p. 56). Circle the benefits that are most meaningful to you. Are there any opportunities still waiting to be grabbed? Mark those as well.

Chapter 4: Your Empty-Nest Marriage

1. As you reflect on your marriage, what are your hopes and dreams for your empty-nest years? Share them with your spouse.
2. What is holding you back from doing whatever is needed to refresh or reboot your relationship?

3. How clear and open is your communication? What can you do to enhance your friendship?

4. Since doing things together is "sexy," consider what adventure you might like to have as a couple. What fits you both?

5. How is the health of your "marriage soul"?

Chapter 5: Rekindling Romance

If you're in a group, allow each other grace to avoid getting too personal on this topic. But be open to discussing Christian counseling services, especially those that specialize in sexual intimacy.

1. Are there any actions you could take to enhance the romance in your marriage? Share your ideas with your spouse.

2. Emotional intimacy precedes good physical intimacy. What does healthy emotional intimacy look like for you?

3. How important to you is having your spouse initiate a time of romance? Have you ever had a conversation about the difference in your libidos (sex drives) and how that relates to your physical intimacy?

4. How do nagging and negativity affect the mood of your physical intimacy? If this is damaging your physical intimacy and closeness, what can you do about it?

5. What hinders you from better sexual intimacy? Be brave and circle which of these eight sex and passion killers affect you the most, then talk with your spouse about what you might do about it.

   a. Exhaustion and stress

   b. Lack of physical affection, flirting, and intimate conversation

   c. Too much to do and too many things left undone

   d. Emotional distance or intense conflict

   e. Lack of safety, emotionally or physically

   f. Feeling unappreciated

   g. Negativity and constant criticism

   h. "Plumbing" isn't working correctly

Chapter 6: Midlife Meltdown or Purposeful Living?

1. When you mix midlife issues with the empty nest, life can get complicated. What five midlife issues are affecting you positively or negatively?

2. Many, though not all, who thrive in midlife have a "now what?" moment. Have you had a "now what?" moment? How have you handled it?

3. What in your life has gone unattended or uncultivated during this stage?

4. What would you say is your passion for life in the empty nest?

5. Do you have any regrets? This question was posed to

people ninety-five years and older. Their top three answers were:

- Reflect more.
- Risk more.
- Do more things that would live on after I'm dead.

Which of these resonates with you most? How would you answer this question?

Chapter 7: Finishing Well

1. Most people don't think much about finishing well until they get to the empty-nest stage of life. What does finishing well mean to you? In your marriage (if married)? With your adult children? With your grandkids? In your faith? In your work?

2. Saint Augustine asked a great question: "What do I wish to be remembered for?" How would you answer?

3. What areas of your life are distracting you from putting more energy into finishing well?

4. According to Celtic tradition, a "thin place" is the thin boundary between heaven and earth. Do you have a thin place in your life where your soul is nourished? What does that look like for you?

5. It seems that people who thrive in the empty nest use their giftedness to serve and make a difference. How are you doing that right now? What would it look like if you put more effort into serving and making a difference?

Chapter 8: Empty-Nest Friendships

1. Do you have safe people and deep friendships in your life? What are you doing to enhance those relationships?
2. "A great life requires great friends." What are the qualities you have found in great friendships?
3. Do you believe you are spending enough time fostering replenishing relationships? If not, what holds you back?
4. Do you have friends with whom you feel safe confessing your mistakes and have an accountability relationship? Has there been a time in your life when you confessed something to a friend and sensed healing taking place?
5. If you are involved in a small group, what is the best part of that group? If you are not in a small group, what is holding you back?

Chapter 9: Single Parent, Empty Nest

1. If you are a single parent living in the empty nest, what part of this chapter is most helpful? What would you like to have added to this chapter?
2. At least two major upheavals take place in a single parent's life: divorce or the death of a spouse and when the adult child leaves home. How do both upheavals relate to each other?
3. How have finances affected your empty-nest experience?

4. As you move forward, it's important to remember that even though life is different, your children haven't totally left your life. What can you do to enhance your relationships with your adult children?

5. Now that the last child is gone, how have you reactivated your social life? What decisions have you made about dating and remarriage?

Chapter 10: How to Be the Grooviest Grandparent in Town

1. How do you feel about the phrase "grandparenting is a marvelous love affair between generations"?

2. Have you decided to invest in your legacy with your grandkids? How are you doing that?

3. What steps can you take to offer blessings (like those described in the chapter) to your grandchildren?

4. Have you had to grandparent during tough times? How has that felt? What have you learned through the experience?

5. Connection with your grandkids is critical. Depending on whether you are a long-distance grandparent or live nearby, your actions may be a bit different. What practical things are you doing to stay bonded with your grandkids?

NOTES

1. Jennifer Pearson, "'I Fell into the Deepest Depression': Madonna Says That Sending Her Daughter Lourdes, 18, to College Was 'Devastating' on Ellen Show," DailyMail.com, March 17, 2015, www.dailymail.co.uk/tvshowbiz/article -2999107.
2. Quoted in John C. Maxwell, *Developing the Leader within You* (Nashville: Thomas Nelson, 1993), 98.
3. For a comprehensive look, check out my book and course *Doing Life with Your Adult Children: Keep Your Mouth Shut and the Welcome Mat Out* (Grand Rapids: Zondervan, 2019).
4. Peter F. Drucker, *The Practice of Management* (New York: HarperCollins, 1986), 147.
5. Anne Lamott, *Traveling Mercies: Some Thoughts on Faith* (New York: Anchor, 2000), 134.
6. Jill Savage, *Empty Nest, Full Life: Discovering God's Best for Your Next* (Chicago: Moody, 2019), 42.
7. Richard Fry, "For First Time in Modern Era, Living with Parents Edges Out Other Living Arrangements for 18- to 34-Year-Olds," Pew Research Center, May 24, 2016, www .pewresearch.org/social-trends/2016/05/24/for-first-time -in-modern-era-living-with-parents-edges-out-other-living -arrangements-for-18-to-34-year-olds/.

8. I deal with this concept more fully in my book *Have Serious Fun: And Twelve Other Principles to Make Each Day Count* (Grand Rapids: Zondervan, 2021).

9. Peter F. Drucker, *The Effective Executive: The Definitive Guide* (New York: HarperCollins, 2006), 24.

10. For more information on decluttering, look through some of the excellent books, blogs, and resources available online by searching on the words *declutter* and *minimalist*.

11. Sonja Haller, "Having Kids Does Make You Happier, but Only after They Leave the Nest, Study Finds," *USA Today*, August 20, 2019, www.usatoday.com/story/life/parenting/2019/08/20/empty-nest-parents-happier-when-kids-move-out-study-finds/2052323001/.

12. Renee Stepler, "Led by Baby Boomers, Divorce Rates Climb for America's 50+ Population," Pew Research Center, March 9, 2017, www.pewresearch.org/fact-tank/2017/03/09/led-by-baby-boomers-divorce-rates-climb-for-americas-50-population/.

13. David Arp and Claudia Arp, *The Second Half: Facing the Eight Challenges of the Empty-Nest Years* (Grand Rapids: Zondervan, 1996), 135.

14. *Shenandoah*, directed by Andrew V. McLaglen, written by James Lee Barrett (Universal Pictures, 1965).

15. Georgia Witkin, "How to Keep Intimacy Alive," *Parade* (April 4, 1993), 12.

16. Mary Jenson, *Taking Flight from the Empty Nest* (Eugene, OR: Harvest House, 2001), 152.

17. Melissa T. Shultz, *From Mom to Me Again: How I Survived My First Empty-Nest Year and Reinvented the Rest of My Life* (Naperville, IL: Sourcebooks, 2016), 133.

18. Frederick Buechner, *Wishful Thinking: A Seeker's ABC* (San Francisco: HarperOne, 1993), 107.

19. Lucille Williams, *The Intimacy You Crave: Straight Talk*

about Sex and Pancakes (Uhrichsville, OH: Shiloh Run Press, 2019), 2.

20. Chrisanna Northrup, Pepper Schwartz, and James Witte, *The Normal Bar: The Surprising Secrets of Happy Couples and What They Reveal about Creating a New Normal in Your Relationship* (New York: Harmony Books, 2012).

21. Bob Buford, *Halftime: Changing Your Game Plan from Success to Significance* (Grand Rapids: Zondervan, 1994), 64.

22. This story is told in Bob Buford's excellent book *Halftime: Changing Your Game Plan from Success to Significance* (Grand Rapids: Zondervan, 1994).

23. Quoted in Buford, *Halftime*, 18.

24. I realize many of my readers do not share my biblical worldview. I'm always so honored that you would read my thoughts anyway.

25. Angela Duckworth, *Grit: The Power of Passion and Perseverance* (New York: Scribner, 2016).

26. For more on engaging with your soul, I recommend John Ortberg, *Soul Keeping: Caring for the Most Important Part of You* (Grand Rapids: Zondervan, 2014).

27. Parker J. Palmer, *On the Brink of Everything: Grace, Gravity, and Getting Old* (Oakland, CA: Barrett-Koehler, 2018), 45.

28. Palmer, *On the Brink of Everything*, 39.

29. Julianne Holt-Lunstad, "So Lonely I Could Die," American Psychological Association, August 5, 2017, www.apa.org/news/press/releases/2017/08/lonely-die.

30. G. Oscar Anderson, "Loneliness among Older Adults: A National Survey of Adults 45+," AARP Research, September 2010, www.aarp.org/research/topics/life/info-2014/loneliness_2010.html.

31. John Townsend, *How to Be a Best Friend Forever: Making and Keeping Lifetime Relationships* (Brentwood, TN: Worthy, 2011), 42.

32. Carol Brzozowski, *Empty Nest, Single Parent: Moving the Needle toward a Repurposed Life* (self-published, 2018), 3.

33. Brzozowski, *Empty Nest, Single Parent*, 9.

34. Jim Burns and Doug Fields, *Getting Ready for Marriage: A Practical Road Map for Your Journey Together* (Colorado Springs: Cook, 2014), 25.

35. Burns and Fields, *Getting Ready for Marriage*, 26–40.

36. Tim Kimmel and Darcy Kimmel, *Extreme Grandparenting: The Ride of Your Life!* (Carol Stream, IL: Tyndale, 2007), 12–13.

37. This, of course, is not the case for the 11 percent of grandparents (almost 3 million in the United States) who, because of a host of issues, are raising their grandchildren.

38. Kimmel and Kimmel, *Extreme Grandparenting*, 84.

39. Jim Burns and Jeremy Lee, *Pass It On: Building a Legacy of Faith for Your Children through Practical and Memorable Experiences* (Colorado Springs: Cook, 2015).

40. Larry Fowler, *Overcoming Grandparenting Barriers: How to Navigate Painful Problems with Grace and Truth* (Minneapolis: Bethany House, 2019), 12.

41. Quoted in Trude B. Feldman, "Colin Powell at Sixty-Five: A Dynamic Statesman," in "In Honor of Secretary of State Colin Powell's Sixty-Fifth Birthday," *Congressional Record* 148, no. 57, May 8, 2002, www.govinfo.gov/content/pkg/CREC-2002-05-08/html/CREC-2002-05-08-pt1-PgS4057-3.htm.

42. Wayne Rice, *Long-Distance Grandparenting: Nurturing the Faith of Your Grandchildren When You Can't Be There in Person* (Minneapolis: Bethany House, 2019), 13.